REVIVAL
PRAYING

BY LEONARD RAVENHILL

Revival God's Way
Revival Praying
Why Revival Tarries

REVIVAL PRAYING

Leonard Ravenhill

BETHANYHOUSE
Minneapolis, Minnesota

Published by Bethany House Publishers
11400 Hampshire Avenue South
Bloomington, Minnesota 55438

Bethany House Publishers is a division of
Baker Publishing Group, Grand Rapids, Michigan.

Printed in the United States of America

Library of Congress Cataloging-in-Publication Data

Ravenhill, Leonard.
    Revival praying: an urgent and powerful message for the family of Christ / by Leonard Ravenhill.
        p.   cm.
    Summary: "Prayer becomes "faith in action" in this enduring classic about how the prayers of a nation can lead to revival"— Provided by publisher.
    ISBN 0-7642-0031-3 (pbk.)
    1. Revivals. 2. Intercessory prayer—Christianity. I. Title.
    BV3793.R28   2005
    248.3'2—dc22

                                                              2004029179

LEONARD RAVENHILL was born in 1907 in the city of Leeds, in Yorkshire, England. After his conversion to Christ, he was trained for the ministry at Cliff College. It soon became evident that evangelism was his forte, and he engaged in it with both vigor and power. Eventually he became one of England's foremost outdoor evangelists. His meetings in the war years drew traffic-jamming crowds in Britain, and great numbers of his converts not only followed the Savior into the kingdom but also into the Christian ministry and the world's mission fields. He emigrated to the United States in midlife, where he continued his ministry. He and his wife, Martha, raised three sons. Ravenhill went home to be with the Lord in November 1994.

LEONARD RAVENHILL, MY FATHER

My mother was a singing mother. Every day as she carried me in her womb she sang and prayed for me. She and Granny, who lived next door to us, prayed together about the child that was to be born. An amazing thing happened two hours—not two months, not two weeks, not two days—after I was born. I was in a prayer meeting. My mother told me twenty years after, "When the midwife went out, I reached over the bed and laid my hands on you and just prayed, 'Lord, make this boy a preacher or don't let him live.'"

The above is a transcript of a forgotten tape that I was given only a matter of days ago in which my father recalls some of his early years. He was raised in a God-fearing home that believed in the power of prayer. His earliest recollection of school was that of being taught the Ten Commandments as a five-year-old as well as having to memorize and recite many of the Psalms. At the age of fourteen he was attending all-night prayer meetings—a passion he carried throughout his life.

He recalled: "They prayed with tears, they prayed with brokenness. They prayed for a lost world, then they began to pray for nations I knew little about. They had signs of Niagara Falls, but instead of water falling over, it was people dropping down."

My father's ministry started in England at the age of sixteen. His burden for the lost took him into the streets, where he began to preach to the local gypsy community—seventy-one years later he was on the streets of Glory.

My father was a powerfully anointed preacher who could bring down the convicting presence of God in a way that very few can. People would begin making their way to the altar even before any type of invitation was given, their hearts pierced by the Word of God. His preaching was superceded only by his passion for prayer. Like the apostle Paul, he carried "the daily pressure of concern for the church." Prayer was his life. Prior to his death in 1994 he told me he had received a number of requests from seminary students who wanted to come and see him for the sole purpose of having him lay his hands upon them in order to receive his "mantle." With his typical dry British humor, but at the same time deadly serious, he said, "Everyone wants to have my mantle but nobody wants my sackcloth and ashes." Sitting at his bedside only days after the stroke that was to take his life, I wrote these words:

Tribute to a Godly Man

I knew a man who gave his life
To see revival fire
He prayed by day, he prayed by night
to birth this one desire.

He had but one obsession
To see a glorious bride
Arrayed in spotless purity
Brought to her bridegroom's side.

His power while in the pulpit
Was matched by very few
And yet he loved the closet
There with the God he knew.

While others strove for man's applause
For fortune and for fame
He had but one ambition
To exalt his Master's name.

For eighty-seven years
He lived just for eternity
A man of faith and wisdom
And true humility.

He knew one day he'd have to stand
Before God's judgment seat
And so he ran to win the prize
His mission to complete.

The fortune that he left behind
Was not in stocks or gold
But lives transformed and challenged—
Their stories yet untold.

There is no greater privilege
Than this that I have had
Of knowing this great man of God
And having him as Dad.

—DAVID RAVENHILL,
AUTHOR AND ITINERANT TEACHER
LINDALE, TEXAS

To
T. A. Hegre
(Affectionately Known as Ted)
An Able Administrator
A Zealous Teacher
A Delightful Friend
This Book
Is
Dedicated
With
My
Gratitude and Affection.

CONTENTS

FOREWORD

"The burden of the Lord" is the statement often used by prophets in the Old Testament age. They were men of God who were aware of the circumstances round about them, of the condition of their people; and they also knew the justice of Almighty God. Therefore, they were aware that the nation which was departing from the truth of God would come into divine judgment. As a result they were deeply burdened, and by the inspiration of God's Spirit they were constrained to cry out against the sins of the people and for true penitence toward God.

The heart of God still yearns over mankind with the same question that He spoke through His servant Ezekiel: "Why will ye die?" The Holy Spirit is still calling upon mankind to turn from the ways of wickedness and return to the Most High, for He is merciful and ready to forgive.

The Holy Spirit uses the channel of prayer in revival ministry. That lesson we have learned from the past and can learn it experientially anew in this day of darkness and spiritual distress. From the burdened heart of a man of God came these burning pages to call God's people to the "effectual, frevent prayer . . . [that] availeth much."

V. Raymond Edman
President
Wheaton College

PREFACE

Bees gather from many flowers. In the course of my reading over the years, I must have stored lots of thoughts in the subconscious mind. These have come out again in different phrases in this writing. Where I could, I have given due acknowledgment to writers.

Concerning my title, the theological purists will probably hound me for marrying these two words *prayer* and *revival*, but after prayer and thought I could do no other. My critics will point out with painful accuracy that while prayer is a New Testament word, revival is not mentioned there. They will be icily correct in their diagnosis. However, I shall retaliate with the irrefutable fact that if revival is not mentioned by direct word of inspiration, it is in the New Testament by inspired inference. Who can deny that revival is in the Acts of the Apostles, and that in the same book praying is wedded to the revivals?

My old master, Samuel Chadwick, had some barbed phrases in his lectures, sermons, and talks. I can still hear his mellow voice saying, "Brethen, the crying sin of the Church is her laziness after God." Praying people, however, are *not* lazy. Prayer demands will power. Prayer recognizes unfinished business with and for God. Prayer is a battle for full-grown men, fully armed and fully awake to the possibilities of grace. I write here by constraint, for my spirit is sore, my heart sick at the slothfulness with which we tarry in prayer. My head hangs low that Communists will give more for their *dying* cause than we will give for the *living* Christ.

I write not for those who want a "bottle" ("I have fed you with milk") but for those who want to battle. My heart is at rest—but I am restless for revival. I have peace—but yet am at war against principalities and powers and against everything in the Church that clutters up the blocked channel through which revival could come. I am not alone, thank God, for many saints long for Christ's appearing—first in the power of revival, and then in majesty in the skies. To them I write these simple words, for such they are. May God bless them to your hungry hearts.

Leonard Ravenhill
December 1961

It has often been said that prayer is the greatest force in the universe. This is no exaggeration. It will bear constant repetition. In this atomic age when forces are being released that stagger the thought and imagination of man, it is well to remember that prayer transcends all other forces. —F. J. Huegel

If the church would only awaken to her responsibility of intercession, we could well evangelize the world in a short time. It is not God's plan that the world be merely evangelized ultimately. It should be evangelized in every generation. There should be a constant gospel witness in every corner of the world so that no sinner need close his eyes in death without hearing the gospel, the good news of salvation through Christ. —T. A. Hegre

CHAPTER ONE

REVIVAL IS IMPERATIVE!

While millions were watching with thumping hearts, American scientists hurled a man into space in May of this year. The same day thousands of souls were launched into a Christless eternity and are in orbit forever in the regions of the damned. Few hearts thumped over their eternal misery; no banner headlines of the press screamed of the eternal woe of those who can never again pass this way.

At the same time as the Red Stone Rocket hurled Commander Shephard into space, there was another launching, maybe of greater value to this sick age. Louis Mumford's book, *The City in History*, was flung into the literary firmament. Displaying Clifton Fadiman's critique of this book, the New York *Times* said, "It is the work of a scholar, philosopher, prophet. If those who run our sorry world (including the average citizen) could be persuaded to absorb its lessons, we might still be able to transform our cities from the obscene hives they are rapidly becoming into places fit for men and women to live." That statement is quite a mouthful and a terrible indictment upon a

15

generation that majors upon physical hygiene, yet wallows in the hog-mire of sexual laxity.

While the pulpit is almost silent, the press is almost eloquent about this sex-intoxication. High pay for low living was never more publicized than in the recent Oscar Awards (the crowns the film stars covet). The best film received a crown for showing the adulterous use of a bedroom; the best actress award went to a siren who played the part of a prostitute; the male crown was given for a star (so-called) who portrayed an evangelist practicing rape instead of preaching redemption. All these details were plastered over the whole world in ten thousand newspapers in a hundred different languages. There is no cover-up now. This thing is out in the open. Christian (?) America is selling soiled sex as a top-line money spinner.

Can you wonder that the Mr. Facing-Both-Ways attitude of the Christian nations puzzles the heathen? Now do you see why Jim Frankel, columnist for the Cleveland Press, says, "If and when American civilization collapses, historians of a future date can look back and sneer, 'They entertained themselves to death' "? If you prefer such a condemnation in an ecclesiastical flavor, well, here is Dr. Tozer saying, "America is laughing her way to hell." This leads me to believe that now is the hour for the church of Rome to find within her tarnished walls another Savanarola. The Europeans need another Luther. England needs another Wesley. America's time is overdue for another Lincoln to be born, who shall clear its pits of obscenity (its night clubs) from the slavery of lust. There is, in my judgment, complete justification for the biting statement, "This is a frustrating time for America; the world is going to hell in a hurry." So said Fred W. Friendly, CBS reporter in *Newsweek*, May 8, 1961.

In July we heard Dr. Billy Graham in a great rally at the State Fair Grounds in Minneapolis, Minnesota. In a statistical review he said that in America there were eight million alcoholics last year. He further quoted that in America in the same year "there were half a million abortions—many among teen-agers," and "some 220,000 illegitimate births, a large proportion among girls in high schools." Criminal abortion is considered the third biggest racket in the United States (*Saturday Evening Post*, May 27, 1961, page 49). These statistics—plus the increasing crime and the added waves of brutality and violence—add up to a frightening total. Yet against this staggering backdrop of iniquity, we hear the voice of the Lord saying, "God willeth not the death of one sinner but rather that all should return, repent, and live."

A writer in an American magazine recently had this to say, "The Reverend——, Bishop of——, recently startled many United States churchgoers when he declared that he does *not* believe in the Biblical account of the virgin birth of Christ. 'It is a primitive religious myth,' he says, 'and Joseph, Mary's husband, was probably the physical father of Jesus.' Asked to name other religious myths, the Dean mentioned Adam and Eve, the Garden of Eden, as well as the existence of a sky-high heaven and a red-hot hell. The Dean's revolt has made many a Protestant congregation sit up and take sharp notice of the fact that a new kind of young man seems to be answering the call to the ministry. If the 47-year-old Dean is a harbinger of the new clergyman, what will tomorrow's Protestant minister be like? What kind of sermons will ring from the pulpit a few years from now, we wonder? In what strange vineyards will we be asked to labor in God's name?"

All over America the strident voice of this theological upstart is heard, for he is written up in countless magazines. He has a right to his opinion, but that does not make his opinion right. He is a spiritual infant crying for a light in the night, a classical example of a theological high-brow lost in the jungle of modern religious thinking. He is a theological hoodlum, intent on wrecking what *is*, and trying to substitute what *isn't*. (He cannot quite explain what that "isn't" is.) Here is a man in the midstream of life who has spent his years hewing out theological cisterns which he now finds hold no water. He has pushed the panic button in the Church of —— and is hoping for the best. This much is sure: Mr. Khrushchev and every Communist in the world will agree with him! I don't think he will be snowed under with letters from Mormons, Russellites, or followers of Father Divine, belligerently assailing him for his denials.

When Dean—— does rise out of his theological rubble, he will discover that he is not the harbinger of a new clergyman for our generation. Actually he is a hangover from the higher criticism of two centuries ago. He is a fellow traveler with Bradlaugh of England, Voltaire of France, and Ingersoll of America, wearing clerical attire. They, too, denied the virgin birth of

Christ, laughed the story of Adam and Eve out of court, and denied the existence of what Dean—— called "the sky-high heaven and a red-hot hell."

One has cause to thank God that a louder voice than this is crying in America today. It must be right to say that in the political and religious realms in America at this hour, the two most popular men are the ex-president of America, Mr. Eisenhower, and Dr. Billy Graham. Thank God that Billy Graham eclipses the Dean by both his voice and his spiritual stature!

In this confused hour of modern living I offer this chapter as a basis for those things which need to cause us deep heart-searching. At this moment there seems to be every justification to cry in the words of old, "Woe to the inhabiters of the earth and of the sea, for the devil is come down"; and again, "The wall is broken down and the gates thereof burned with fire." The alternative may not be Christ *or* chaos; it may be Christ *and* chaos. I well remember a lady in New Zealand saying recently that she feared to pray for revival because national revival seems to be a prelude to coming judgment. Maybe she is right, but better to have revival followed by judgment than to have judgment without a revival preparation.

In Luke 15, one conspicuous failure in the life of the elder brother was that he measured his own goodness by the badness of his prodigal brother. He should have seen how low he too had sunk in lacking compassion for a lost soul; he should have recognized how low he himself had fallen from the height of concern his father lived on. He should have known that the prodigal son did not need to come home. He had alternatives. He could have floated a loan and gone back to the gaming tables, hoping for a change in fortunes. He could have changed his job, arguing that he was just upset because pig-raising was not his line. Or worse still, he could have committed suicide.

Have we Christians dropped into the sin of the elder brother? Are we who still have coals of fire on our altars measuring ourselves by the fireless altars of neighboring churches instead of checking on the praying blaze of our saintly forbears? The world boasts its atomic power; some cults boast their satanic power; but where are those who boast Holy Ghost power?

In God's name I ask, Why do men wander in the wilderness of this world while in our churches we have room to seat them all and to spare? Yet they do *not* come to church. There are reasons for this. Is the failure in the pulpit? Paul Althus said, "People today are not tired of preaching but tired of *our* preaching." Does he mean the pulpit has form but not fire, doctrine but not dynamic? Does he infer that the church has a spire, but does not aspire to holiness? Does he mean that most of us church folk are sanctimonious, but not sanctified? Do we wince when we recall the biting sneer of Nietzsche. "You will have to *look* more redeemed if I am to believe in your Redeemer"? Helmut Thielicke puts it this way: "When we come from church, we give the impression that instead of coming from the Father's banquet. we have just come from a sheriff who has auctioned off our sins, and now we

are sorry that we can't get them back again." If
any or all of these accusations and suggestions are
true, I believe the failure stems back to our poverty in
prayer. To offer different brands of politics as a
cure-all for this sick age is like handing out aspirins
to incurable cancer patients. A few nights ago when
I had the pleasure of having dinner with the top-line
ministers of our city, they were still glowing after
Billy Graham's campaign here. A Presbyterian minister,
who was obviously greatly moved, spoke for all of us
as he said, "Brethren, America must have revival
or she is sunk."

America does not need Russia to humble her, for
she has lost face over an apple-sized island at her
toe (Cuba). America does not need Russia to break
her, for she is breaking herself on the bosses of God's
truth. Some say that Barry Goldwater could bring
America back to the old American way of life.
A bigger issue is this: Can America remain free
another four years before the next election? Can she
stave off financial ruin as long as she has evaded
moral collapse?

Five minutes *before* Elijah appeared on the scene,
no one had any idea that he was in the offing; five
minutes *after* he came in the power of the Spirit, a
nation knew "there was a man sent from God."
The Church of God today is an island surrounded
with the gods of Baal. Voltaire, though wrong in most
of what he said, was right, I think, in this statement:
"History is the sound of soft, silken slippers coming
down the stairs, and the thunder of hobnail boots
going up." Hark the thunder of those boots in America!

Sinned as we have as a nation, yet to our sin we have added pride in our sinning. The world has lost the power to blush over its vice; the Church has lost her power to weep over it.

Do you ask, "Well now, where do we go from here?" The answer is, "Where sinful individuals or sinful nations can only go—back to a merciful God." Hear me! Every church without a prayer meeting condemns us; every Bible daily unopened condemns us; every promise of God unused condemns us; every lost neighbor condemns us; every lost heathen condemns us; every dry eye among us condemns us; every wasted minute of our time condemns us; every unclaimed opportunity for God condemns us. Next year is not ours. Tomorrow may be too late. Unless we repent *now*, unless we return and fire the prayer altars *now*, unless we fast and weep *now*, woe unto us at the judgment!

Inspire the living faith,
  Which whosoe'er receives
The witness in himself he hath
  And consciously believes—
The faith that conquers all,
  And doth the mountain move,
And saves whoe'er on Jesus calls,
  And perfects them in love.
                    —Charles Wesley (1750)

Wherefore also we pray always for you, that our God would count you worthy of this calling, and fulfill all the good pleasure of his goodness, and the work of faith with power (II Thess. 1:1). This prayer is for success to every practical enterprise of faith, as well as for the satisfaction of every aspiration and desire after moral excellence.
                    —Moffatt, Expositor's Greek New Testament

CHAPTER TWO

PRAYER—FAITH OPERATING

Preachers and politicians are flinging sobering words around to describe the peril of this hour which is so dark morally, spiritually, and politically. No longer is Communism merely creeping over the earth, but rather it is leaping over it. Khrushchev is no longer whispering his dark secrets in secret; he is shouting them by radio over housetops and hilltops. Communism is no longer just a tavern subject bantered about by moral and intellectual derelicts; to millions, it has become a respectable fellow traveler on the road of life. No longer is the Marxist gang a down-at-the-heel, ragged minority; it is a well-dressed society, at least amongst many of its leaders, and the Marxist philosophy maneuvers some of the greatest scientific brains in the world, though we do not quite know how. No more are the Bolsheviks an over-the-wall group of upstarts, sneered at by old-time demagogues and democrats; now they sit at the conference tables of world councils, not asking questions but stating policies, not just bartering but belligerent. This black cancer of Communism has spread until it covers almost three-quarters of the earth's surface. It is estimated that in some way or other it taints nearly two out of every three persons. If the Lord tarries and there is no revival of pure Christianity, then the next span of years will be the worst that history has ever recorded.

Tactics hitherto unknown to politicians are being used in this day to stir up international enmity. A radio announcer the other night said that Mr. Khrushchev had offered to stop talking about America's U2 spying episode if America would forget to mention Russia's rape of Hungary! (Has Russia a guilt complex in this?) The Christian Church as such has not organized military opposition to Communism. Yet the Communists have murdered millions of true Christians, and during the Korean massacres have written a page of grim horror in martyrdom, equalling the atrocities of *Fox's Book of Martyrs*. The next span of years we could well describe in the words of Bertrand Russell as "500 years of Genghis Khan." Brunner calls this description of Russell's "a typical English understatement," for "first of all, the advance of the world-conquering Mongols of Central Asia was stopped decisively in the year 1241 at Liegnitz; the Genghis Khan world domination applied only to the people of the East; moreover, its tyranny cannot even vaguely be compared to the tyranny of a modern totalitarian state, especially the tyranny of the Communist system. In the foreseeable future, there is no immediate hope that the strangle grip of communism will be broken."

When the old-time Russian dramatist Gogol spoke of "mankind with *dead* souls," he was describing exactly that which modern nations are without God. Another writer speaks of the growth of militant godlessness in the world today until the world is swarming with human beings no longer human but just "beings." Frightful thought! After Communist brainwashing and indoctrination ("correct" indoctrination), we shall have a nation or generation of robots. Communism can create millions of zombies, after having spared only a few thousands of people who would be needed as the ruling class. Communism is versatile and devastating. Its leaders have declared that they can take America without firing a shot, and top-line politicians seem to agree with them.

All this adds up to a terrifying picture. Well might we cry, "Watchman, what of the night?" Never was there a need for the trumpeters on Zion's walls to sound a louder blast to sleeping believers than at this moment. Many Christians right now are hanging their harps on the willows and crying, "How shall we sing the Lord's song in a strange land?"

Ours is the hour for men of faith. In the Old Testament the three Hebrew children had a defiant faith. They cried, "Our God. . . *is able* to deliver us from the burning fiery furnace." Of God's *ability* they had no doubt, though of His *plan* they were not quite sure. As a matter of fact God did not choose to deliver them *from* the furnace but *in* it. Their faith, however, had gone beyond getting into the fire. They said, "Our God. . . is able to deliver us from the burning fiery furnace, *but if not*, be it known unto thee, O king, that we will not. . . serve thy gods nor worship the golden image." Their faith believed when it could not see. In the New Testament days iron gates yielded to an angel's touch when prayer was made without ceasing unto God for Peter.

On the one hand, faith is a tender plant, easily bruised; on the other hand, faith is also as sturdy as an oak that will not bow before a gale.

"O for a faith that will not shrink
Though pressed by many a foe,
That will not tremble on the brink
Of poverty or woe."

Often we hear the prayer, "Lord, Thou art *able* to do this." That prayer is very good and may build up confidence in the pray-er. But—and this is important—*to say* "God is able" is not faith. Here is a simple but imperfect picture of our lack these days: I myself believe that the God who once turned water into wine is *able* to turn into pure gold the desk on which I am writing. (It is sixty inches by thirty-four inches.) What a wonderful slab of gold it would make! What good outlets for the money which the gold would bring me! But—and here is where I fail—I do not have the faith to believe that God *will* turn this desk into gold. My theology says that God *can* do it, but on the faith end I fail. I have said before that one of these days someone will read the Bible for the first time, believe it, and act on it with a daring, simple faith. Then we long-time believers will bow in shame, crying, "Lord, help our unbelief."

Faith honors God. God honors faith and goes wherever faith puts Him. Faith, Biblical faith, can do all that God can do. (Because its sole desire is God's glory, it would not ask any thing amiss—I John 5:14.) Faith's supreme longing is for the return of the glory that has departed from the sanctuary. Its ambition is not colored by the clay vessel. Faith is wedded to the love which "seeketh not her own." Faith longs for an overthrow of the powers of darkness. Faith yearns that the world might know the message of redeeming love, and aches for enslaved millions to be unfettered from the chains of sin. Faith has compassion for those

"Bound, who should conquer——
Slaves, who should be kings."

This present day is like an arena whose terraces are filled with the militant godless, the brilliant and belligerent skeptics, plus the blank-faced heathen millions, all looking into the empty ring to see what the Church of the living God can do. How I burn at this point! What are we Christians doing? To use a very tattered phrase, are we just "playing church"? With all our revival campaigns, are we getting folk into Biblical regeneration? Is it really a comfort to know that the recent converts will become just like us? What if they are as lazy and self-excusing in the matter of personal devotion to Jesus and active engagement in soul-winning as the rest of our listed church members? Is that a thrilling thought? Or is it a spine-chilling one? If "like produces like," does this prospect of the new additions to the church furrow our brows or flood our hearts with joy? Surely we need some new injection into the Church of the living God immediately. Since that Church is composed of mortal men and women, it means that we need some new dynamic.

The path to this new individual and collective power would be as follows: first, renunciation of all known sin; secondly, sorrowful confession that we have failed so much and have been satisfied so long with the

status quo; thirdly, a seeking of God's face in earnest
prayer; and finally, Bible study, in order to uncover the
promises of God directed to this desperate age and our
needy churches.

Natural faith—natural man's believing in something
that has not been done before—has driven men to great
heights of accomplishment. Without natural faith could
Cortez have conquered Mexico? How could Hannibal
have crossed the Alps without it? If Columbus had not
had this faith to do what seemed impossible, what could
he have done in the face of near mutiny on the high
seas? Had men not had faith—natural faith—neither
the Parthenon nor the Pyramids would be standing.

Spiritual faith cannot be kept in a watertight com-
partment of the mind. Faith gets into the will and
into the heart. Faith sets the affections on fire. Spiritual
faith can and must ignite ambition—spiritual ambition,
I mean. I think of the Maréchale, who went into an
old basement in Paris to establish the Salvation Army
in France. This task was no ball. It was a herculean
task. This frail, cultured, young English lady was
tackling a man-sized job. She was fired with ambition
to tread down Satan's domain in the triumphant power
of the risen Son of God. And she, with others, did it;
they came out "more than conquerors."

One great value of reading the Word of God
is that it is faith-feeding, for "faith cometh by
hearing, and hearing by the word of God." Notice
that it does not say that faith cometh by reading or that
faith cometh by seeing. Faith comes by hearing. The
soul has "ears" (Gal. 3:5). Jesus Christ said, "He that

hath *an ear*, let him *hear* what the Spirit *saith*." (It is present tense, for the Spirit still speaks to the inner ear of the heart.) In the place of prayer, the soul also has eyes which "see." In the place of prayer, the soul has aspirations which are sanctified and set aflame and, what is more, kept aflame. Do you wonder that the devil strives with might and main with all that is reasonable—and all that is unreasonable too—to keep us from this soul-hearing, soul-seeing, soul-activating place of prayer?

Unlimited access to unlimited wealth would be the undoing of most of us, for what needless, useless (and maybe worthless) things many of us would buy. How prodigal we would be in operating that hoard! Would we be less foolish if there were unconditional approach to God with unconditional resources involved?

For some thirty years my father spent every Sunday afternoon visiting the sick in the infirmary at Leeds, England. Through operating the talent God had given him, he led hundreds to Christ. He was particularly successful in winning Catholics to the Saviour. His fulcrum was the Word of the Lord, and his lever his own experience in grace. (He had been an acolyte in the Roman church and knew whereof he spoke.) One day in the course of his hospital visitation, a sick man listened to my father's testimony, then jabbed back at him feelingly with, "I have prayed to God and He did not hear me. Why?"

Dad answered the man this way: "Suppose the king of our country came into this room right now, and I asked him for five pounds (equal to twenty dollars

then), would the king give it to me? After all, I am
a loyal subject of the crown."

The man thought for a moment and then replied,
"I don't suppose that he would give it."

"Well then," Father said, "suppose that after I had
asked the king and had been refused, the Prince
of Wales had come into the room. Would he get the
money he asked for?"

"Oh yes," answered the man, "but then, he's the
king's son."

"Exactly right!" Father said. "Relationship makes
all the difference."

In making a request of God, the first thing we have
to be sure of is this: Is our relationship right? Once
we are convinced by the witness of the Spirit that
we are blood-related to the Father and not at variance
with others, we can come with boldness to the throne
of grace. Soiled hearts that operate soiled hands can
not plunder the resources of God, for God's command
is "Be ye clean that bear the vessels of the Lord."
Assured that we are blood-related to God, and confident
that we are joint-heirs with Christ of the fabulous
riches of God, what manner of persons we ought to be!
Is there any excuse at all for our present poverty?
When He longs to give full vision, is there any reason
why we should still be seeing men as trees walking?
With the promise of the mighty Holy Ghost to empower
us, is there any self-defense when we stagger under the
load and fail to "put to flight the armies of the aliens"?
Has God failed? Is God unwilling to bless? No! Ten
thousand times no!

It is my solemn conviction that the most glorious hour of the Church has yet to be born. All the heroes of faith have not yet been listed. All the chapters of the Church, "fair as the moon, clear as the sun, and terrible as an army with banners," have not yet been written. The greatest exploits of faith have yet to be done. Faith is basic to all that we are in God and to all that we can do for Him. Peter's admonition is "add to your *faith* virtue; and to virtue knowledge." (Notice that the Word does *not* say, "add to your *knowledge* faith.") Faith is the muscle by which we lift the load; faith is the currency by which we make purchases in the spiritual kingdom; faith is spiritual sight. Men of faith see—they see the unseeable. Men of faith know a dimension that is unknown to those who pray only routine prayers. God demands faith, for He says, "Without faith it is *impossible* to please [God]." Faithlessness hurts Christ and also hurts His cause. Jesus himself said, "O faithless. . . generation, how long shall I be with you? How long shall I suffer you?" In E. M. Bounds' great writings, he says: "When faith ceases to pray, it ceases to live." It is also true that when faith ceases to live, it ceases to pray. Faith *must* pray in order to live; faith *must* live in order to pray.

Bahkt Singh told us that while he was speaking one time, a man kept staring at an electric light in the room. Then the man requested Bahkt Singh to lend him the electric bulb. His request was granted. But days later, the man returned, downcast, for the bulb was useless, he said. Thereupon Bahkt Singh went to the man's room to investigate why this almost new bulb would not light. The answer was not hard to find.

The innocent man had taken the bulb and had tied it with a piece of string to the ceiling of the room. He had no electric current; therefore his bulb had no contact with the power supply.

The light bulb for us Christians is prayer, and God has the power. But it is faith that makes the connection!

Is it not a proof that the Holy Spirit is to a great extent a stranger in the church when prayer, for which God has made such provisions, is regarded as a task and a burden? And does not this teach us to seek for the deep root of prayerlessness in our ignorance of and disobedience to the Divine Instructor, whom the Father has commissioned to teach us to pray?

—Andrew Murray

CHAPTER THREE

THE SHAME OF OUR NAKEDNESS

There is one thing we mortals never seem to need to learn—how to make excuses. We have a native ability to offer a reason why for every failure.

The worldly-wise say, "The Church is struggling for survival." One man is bold enough to say the Church is at last "on the way out." Another thinks that she needs to drop some of the barnacles she has picked up in sailing the sea of Time so long, and then undergo a dry-dock operation to convert this old sailing ship into a trim, atom-powered vessel that might call for the respect of the world.

This is old philosophy in new language. The fact is that the Church has been caught naked. She has not the power she talks of, or else she is pitiably sick and cannot display that power. In Scotland, if folk struggling on the poverty line (maybe in the Gorbals in Glasgow) could only prove their pedigree and so claim their inheritance, they *could* be living in some castle in Perth. Such is a correct picture of the Church today, for she trails in poverty when riches in Christ are hers. She seems to be in flight instead of in fight. We have a stricken Church in a stricken world.

But the embarrassing thing right here is that we have no one to blame for our spiritual impotence. We have not half a chance that anyone will believe us for transferring to another the guilt of our criminal stagnation. We cannot blame the devil for this impassé, because Jesus said, "I give unto you power ... over all the power of the enemy." We cannot blame our enemies, because the Word says, "We are more than conquerors through him that loved us." We cannot blame the weapons combined against us, because we have "the shield of faith, wherewith ye shall be able to quench all the fiery darts of the wicked." We dare not and cannot blame God, because He has said, "Ask, and it shall be given you." We cannot say that the supply lines have run out, because the Book says, "All things are yours." It looks as if we have run out of scapegoats! As a wise man said, "The fault, dear Brutus, is within ourselves."

To meet the crisis hour in the Church and in the world today, we either have or do not have what it takes. Consider the Bible story of the importunate friend. It would seem that a certain man had once been in trouble; then a friend got him out of that tight spot. Because of this he promised to be eternally grateful and repay the favor to the friend any time, any where, at any cost. Later, at the worst time and in the worst place, the benefactor was himself in trouble. But he remembered the promise. Although it was midnight, he told himself that he would be welcomed at any hour because of the favor he had given. So bang, bang on the door. Upstairs a man stirred unhappily. Finally he got up, went to the door, and showed his one-time benefactor in. But then he ran back to his wife lamenting, "A friend of mine in his journey hath come to me and *I have nothing to set before him.*" Alas, his cupboard was bare!

This bare cupboard is a far cry from Peter's thrilling words, "Such as I have, give I thee: In the name of Jesus Christ of Nazareth, rise up and walk." In the days of the early Church, organized religion was able to do nothing for the cripple, long wilted at the gate of the temple called Beautiful. But an outcast preacher (Peter) who never had a chance to fill the temple's pulpit, filled this lame man's need. Peter met the need through the Name.

If we today could rediscover the virtue in that Name, the victory in that Name, the violence in that Name, we could set this world alight for God. Most of us have enough grace to scrape through the day, but we have nothing over. We are conquerors but are not *"more* than conquerors." We can fight off the enemy but cannot take any prisoners. Ours is a defense action, not an attacking power.

We are choosy with the Scriptures. We sing lustily, "Every promise in the Book is mine." Well, here's one: "I know thy works [service], that thou art neither cold nor hot: I would thou wert cold or hot. So then because thou art lukewarm and neither cold nor hot, *I will spue thee out of my mouth.*" Are we claiming *this* word too? Are we hot? Are we cold? Are we lukewarm? Are we making God sick (fearful thought!)?

Men say that right can never be wrong and that wrong can never be right. I disagree. Here is a man playing with his lovely baby daughter on the lawn of his home. The birds are singing and the sun is shining. This family man prefers giving joy to his child and getting happiness in romping with her to receiving delight from any ball game. But suddenly, as he is playing, there is the wail of the fire alarm. This father is also on the fire team, and by all the rights of law and humanity, he should leave his child and rush to the nearby fire department. However, he thinks a second time, and I hear him mutter, "Let somebody else take care of the fire this time." Though he is the driver of the fire truck, and though he knows that his absence will delay the take-off of the fire team, yet he decides to stay and play. *Before* the fire alarm went off, he was in the right to play; *after* it went off, he was guilty of criminal negligence that probably cost lives.

Are we Christians playing on the lawn while men perish? This go-to-church-once-a-week-and-pay-your-tithes-and-sing-in-the-choir Christianity is a farce, if that is the limit of our Christian service and the extent of our passion for souls. In this holy war, we who wail about encroaching cults and engulfing Communism are like a crowd of men who have been given all the ammunition needed and all the equipment called for, yet refuse to use it. God pity us!

We *will* learn to pray, I am sure, for God will see to that. He is not concerned about our happiness but about our holiness. In other words, God is concerned that we wear character. Friend in Christ, we have a million millenniums in which to be happy. Because of our lateness in spiritual maturity, most of us have about twenty-five years of life left to serve Christ; then through eternity, bliss. When we have fewer mouth-watering commodities, we will have less time for our feet under the table and more time for our knees on the floor in prayer. When we have less eye-catching TV and less thrilling music, and when we have the spirit of heaviness and know more of poverty than plenty, we might get our foot on the first rung of the ladder of intercession. What fools we are if we have to pay the price of a Communist take-over before we get serious in quitting "playing church" and in getting into the stream of divine anointing for revival in our day!

In the current issue of *Conquest for Christ* (the official organ of International Students, Inc.), there is an article by Bakht Singh. This dear Christian leader in India says, "The indigenous churches in India have a great burden for America just now. . . and are praying that God will visit your country with revival. . . . You feel sorry for us in India because of our poverty in *material* things. We who know the Lord in India feel sorry for you in America because of your *spiritual* poverty. We pray that God may give you gold tried in the fire which He had promised to those who know the power of His resurrection. . . . In our churches we spend four or five or six hours in prayer and worship, and frequently our people wait on the Lord in prayer all night; but in America after you have been in church for one hour, you begin to look at your watches. We pray that God may open your eyes to the true meaning of worship. . . . To attract people to meetings, you have a great dependence on posters, on advertising, on promotion, and on the build-up of a human being; in India we have nothing more than the Lord Himself and we find that He is sufficient. Before a Christian meeting in India we never announce who the speaker will be. When the people come, they come to seek the Lord and not a human being or to hear some special favorite speaking to them. We have had as many as 12,000 people come together just to worship the Lord and to have fellowship together. We are praying that the people in America might also come to church with a hunger for God and not merely a hunger to see some form of amusement or hear choirs or the voice of any man."

Do we get huffed at this voice in India crying against the spiritual poverty of rich America? The strength of Bakht Singh is that what he talks of he has done. He has found that Madison-Avenue-advertising methods and campaign costs (needing a Wall Street behind them) are not related in the least way to New Testament Christianity. Have we strayed too far to get back again to New Testament procedure? Have we? Such a question permits no easy answer.

There is no power like that of prevailing prayer—of Abraham pleading for Sodom, Jacob wrestling in the stillness of the night, Moses standing in the breach, Hannah intoxicated with sorrow, David heartbroken with remorse and grief, Jesus in sweat of blood. Add to this list from the records of the church your personal observation and experience, and always there is the cost of passion unto blood. Such prayer prevails. It turns ordinary mortals into men of power. It brings power. It brings fire. It brings rain. It brings life. It brings God. —Samuel Chadwick

CHAPTER FOUR

A CLASSIC OLD TESTAMENT PRAYER

Someone has said, "When God wanted to get a man, He had to get a woman first." This was certainly true of Hannah, a sure picture of a "mother in Israel." Here is a person sold out to one thing. Here is a soul chastised by barrenness and chastened by the abundance of another. To Hannah, every cry of joy or of pain from Peninnah's children must have been like a sword-thrust. Moreover, there must have been a wearing down in her situation, because the Scripture says that it was year after year that Hannah's adversary, Peninnah, "provoked her sore" when she went up into the house of the Lord. Years Hannah waited! Years Hannah wept! Years Hannah suffered reproach! Years she was grieved!

What twisted ideas we get about prayer in our day. To many of us prayer is just a short cut to receiving a desired thing. Yet if the Lord tarry, we must wait for His answer. "If Hannah's prayer for a son had been answered at the time she set for herself," said W. E. Biederwolf, "the nation might never have known the mighty man of God that it found in Samuel."

Hannah's prayer is a classic because in it are revealed the true ingredients of intercessory prayer (the highest type of prayer known to believers). In many churches there are warriors in prayer, and these gather collectively to fight the good fight of faith; others just pray. But true intercessors "stand in the gap" until through them comes the answer.

Hannah shared a home and shared a husband but could not share the children, for she was barren. There hung her shame. Note the increasing intensity in the order of events in Hannah's prayer vigil. Hannah prayed (I Sam. 1:10), continued praying (vs. 12), and finally "poured out [her] soul" (vs. 15). Hannah wept (vs. 8), but later she wept sore (vs. 10). Because of her barren state, Hannah was grieved (vs. 10) and "in bitterness of soul" (vs. 10). She regarded her unproductive state as an affliction, which she classified as "my complaint and grief" (vs. 16). Finally, after fasting from food and drink (vs. 8, 15), she made a vow: "O Lord of hosts, if *thou* wilt indeed look on the affliction of thine handmaid, and remember me, and not forget thine handmaid, but wilt give unto thine handmaid a man child, then *I* will give him unto the Lord all the days of his life, and there shall no razor come upon his head" (I Sam. 1:11). All this adds up to a woman desperate to get a remedy for her provoking condition.

This woman could have prayed just for a child. The answer to her prayer would have removed her reproach. But she plays or really prays for higher stakes—"Give unto thine handmaid a *man* child." Hannah wanted a son. To her that was the highest honor. A child would remove her shame, and a *man* child would bring her honor. "But God wanted more than just a man child. God wanted a prophet, and a savior, and a ruler for His people." God did for Hannah far more "exceeding abundantly above all that [she] could ask or think." In solving her problem, He solved His own. He granted her request for a man child (Samuel), but she gave him back to the Lord as she had vowed. Thus, many years later when God needed a man to "stand in the gap" for Israel, He had one in the prophet Samuel.

There are other important observations to make about this great Old Testament story. Hannah offered her own means as a channel through which God could bring deliverance. It was through Hannah herself that the Lord answered her prayer. God took of her flesh and substance to give her the petition she had asked of Him. All she had was geared to give her the child she had asked of God. In the early stages of giving birth to this child, just one part of Hannah knew of the conception; later her whole body felt the weight of that which is natural and yet, to say the least, irregular. In the first part of this miracle no inconvenience was felt in her body; later, this same experience dislocated all her usual manner of life. There were late nights when sleep would not come; there was a throwing aside of the social program; there may have been a distaste for food; and there may have been midnight hours. Later, while others were sleeping, Hannah was still awake because of the near birth of her coveted child. She would not have the situation otherwise.

All this experience can be translated into terms for revival praying. In our day we do not pray that the miracle of revival will simply erase the record of our barrenness. I have said before that prayer not only changes things; prayer changes people. Prayer changed Hannah! She who had been barren became fruitful, and therefore useful and joyful. The same is true of us all in the time of revival. We are inclined to look at dwindling congregations or church seats that have never known a congregation, and to sigh for a revival that would fill them all. That is perhaps better than having no concern at all. But right here we must remember (because it is imperative) that we must be moved with godly jealousy. Hannah could not stand the provocation of her "adversary." It continued year after year. Finally Hannah did something about it.

In Genesis chapter thirty, verse one, we have a like picture. The text reads: "When Rachel saw that she bare Jacob no children, Rachel envied her sister; and said unto Jacob, Give me children, or else I die." That was anguish indeed. All Jacob had done in serving for fourteen years to have Rachel as a wife failed to give comfort. The fact that Jacob loved her more than her rival (who was her sister as well as joint wife, Genesis 29:30), failed to give comfort. Rachel was barren and knew it. Others knew it too. The shame of this barrenness got to be a burden beyond endurance, and in despair she flung herself at the feet of her husband with the shattering cry, "Give me children, or else I die."

Something of this shame must overcome us if we are to see our spiritual desert rejoice and blossom as the rose. Before the Lord will move in power, our orthodoxy will have to be stabbed, our conventions shattered, and our stony hearts again know tears. Only a small portion of the Church will conceive in the Holy Ghost; but later, the whole body of the Church will feel the birth. There will be some nights of prayer, some fasting, and a grief born of anguish at the plight of perishing millions, lost—eternally, irretrievably lost. It has been stated that in this exploding world population, there are more people born into the world in one day than are added to the true Church, which is His body, in one year! Even slight meditation on such a statement makes a disturbing picture.

This much is sure: From the time of conception until the appointed time of deliverance, Hannah had to stay with her precious burden. Alas and alas, this is a rush age. If we could, we would rush God too. We want big blessing for small installments, the birth of revival but not pain of the birth. Sometime, I hope, we are going to get sick of playing church (to use a modern cliché), and get so angry at our birth poverty in the soul realm that we too will sanctify a fast, call a solemn assembly, and seek the face of the Lord.

People often write to me along this strain: "A few of us in our church are concerned for revival. Some of our members ignore us; some openly oppose us; others chill us with their indifference; the pastor seems to take a neutral attitude. What shall we do about this?" I would say, "Read again the story of Hannah."

Apparently Hannah was so distressed that she fasted: "Then said Elkanah her husband to her, Hannah, . . . why eatest thou not?" How did Moses fast forty days and then after his trouble return again and fast another forty days? Are we greater than Moses? How is it that the Son of God fasted alone in the desert? Are we better informed than the Son of God? Why does Paul talk of weariness, painfulness, *fastings?* Have we got a better view of things than had Paul? Paul might get a little rough with us today and say that we are of those "whose god is their belly."

One of the hardest things for Hannah to take in the period of her heart distress was the fact that Eli, the priest of the Lord, completely misunderstood her state. Read it: "Only her lips moved, but her voice was not heard." (There is a time when language is bankrupt, for the highest form of prayer has no speech.) Because of Hannah's silent prayer Eli thought she "had been drunken" (vs. 13). If you get Spirit-intoxicated about revival, if you get to the place where there is little relish for food, somebody is going to start jeering.

Hannah "bare a son, and called his name Samuel. . . . And when she had weaned him, she. . .brought him unto the house of the Lord. . .and the child was young." I can see the face of this dear Hebrew woman when on a certain day each year she went to see the child whom, in keeping with her vow, she had presented to the Lord as a temple watcher. Surely she too said, "My soul doth magnify the Lord."

Some time later the nation Israel decided to go the way of the other nations and have a king. Hear the cry of Hannah's son—not the cry of self-pity, not the cry for self-justification nor for self-restoration. He who had been born for the need of the nation, he who had carried the burden for the nation, now, after many years of service, lays down his *office*, but not his *burden*, with the words, "God forbid that I should sin against the Lord in ceasing to pray for you." Not many men carry their burden after they are pushed out of office. But Samuel had been born of a praying mother—truly a great woman in prayer—and converts often take on the atmosphere in which they are born. (They say some souls born in the spiritual flame that swept the Hebrides found a famous Bible conference in England to be "cold.")

A brother said to me just hours ago, "Brother Len, we can have New Testament revivals whenever we follow the New Testament pattern." I am sure he is right. Moreover, of this I am fully persuaded: *With a once-a-week prayer meeting no church (here or in any other place, at this or at any time) is going to get us a heaven-born, Spirit-operated revival.* Before "Pentecost was fully come," the disciples prayed; and *as they were praying,* the Spirit fell upon them; *after* Pentecost we discover that twenty-eight chapters in Acts mention prayer, for they "continued in prayer," says the record. We need prayer to obtain victory and then prayer to maintain victory. We need to pray about our praying; we must pray unction upon others as they are praying. We must pray alone; we must pray together; we must pray in the night and not cease in the day.

"Lord, teach us to pray!"

Someone has said that faith has three distinct stages:
the faith that reckons,
the faith that rests,
the faith that risks.

CHAPTER FIVE

"DEEP CALLETH UNTO DEEP"

Prayer—protracted prayer, groaning prayer, fasting prayer, weeping prayer, speechless prayer—belongs to those initiated into a spirit of prayer, that is, into "praying in the Holy Ghost." To the uninstructed, terms like these mean "works." But praying friend, faint not; such critics may yet learn. In the language of Horatius Bonar it may be said of protracted, groaning, speechless prayer, "It is the way the Master went. Should not the servant tread it still?"

Dr. Tozer sets forth the new approach and mediation of modern evangelism in a brilliant article, "The Old Cross and the New." I think he could well have added a spicy chapter on our new ways of praying. Isn't it pitiable, regrettable, and indefensible that we try to operate almost all our churches on one "sweet *hour* of prayer"? Yet in actuality, that sweet "hour" is much taken up with Bible study. There certainly has to be Scripture read so that faith may be generated (Rom. 10:17) and we may have God's promises as a foundation for prayer. But after all, the prayer meeting is a *prayer* meeting. The fact that far too many churches are combining the prayer meeting with a Bible study is the church's self-acknowledged prayer weakness. In short, the church is saying that it can *not* hold out in prayer, so it fills in the time with Bible study. Yet no church these days can operate on *one* hour of prayer a week, let alone on the half hour we are giving collectively to intercession. To those who have never developed a prayer life, the demand for time spent in prayer makes all the more strange the description of true prayer mentioned at the beginning of this chapter.

I believe most of us will need the tears wiped from our eyes when the books are opened at the judgment bar of God, and our personal prayer record is read. By a strange paradox those who pray most, feel they pray little. This much is sure: No man who prays, struts!

Prayer is a two-way operation—man talking to God and God talking to man. Solomon was wise when he requested a listening heart (I Kings 3:9, margin). To many, prayer is dry because *they* do all the talking. I remember chatting one day with a teen-ager and asking him, "What is your trouble?"

"I am a backslider," he replied with some heat.

"How do you know you are backslidden?" I countered.

He looked me straight in the eye and said, "Because God doesn't talk back to me anymore!"

Friend, how about you? Does God talk back to you? After the Resurrection, Jesus had been seen by over five hundred brethren at once, and thousands of others had been born of God at and subsequent to Pentecost. Then why, I wonder, was Ananias the Lord's choice of a man to visit a seeking Jew and to "go into the street called Straight to enquire in the house of Judas for one called Saul of Tarsus"? Was it that Ananias had stayed to listen to God and to get directions from the Lord for the day's operations? What Saul of Tarsus do you and I miss contacting because in morning devotions we pray for help just to get through the day and fail to pray for specific guidance in testimony? Without prayer we can *not* live the Christian life. Prayer means power. More prayer means more power.

Recently a racing motorist came within an ace of winning one of the world's greatest motor races, but because he risked going the last lap without checking his gas tank, he failed. Within a few hundred yards of the winning flag, he was stalled. As the competitor who had chased him so long flashed past him to gain the coveted award, the near-winner was chagrined.

The place where the Christian stops to refuel is prayer. Yet it is prayer far beyond "refuelling" that engages us now. In his masterly Epistle to the Romans, Paul talks of the witness of the Spirit (8:16). We Christians have isolated this passage to one single interpretation—the Spirit bearing witness to our justification. But in the Christian's life, the Spirit also bears witness to our praying, as well as to everything else. As a Christian, our Advocate is truly with the Father, and we talk to the Father through the Son. Yet the Father talks to us through the Spirit. Jesus is *our* Advocate, but the Spirit is the Advocate of *God the Father*. The Spirit bore witness to Paul that he had the true burden and spirit of prayer, for Paul says, "My conscience... bearing me *witness in the Holy Ghost*" (Rom. 9:1). How often, if ever, do we stop to see whether the Holy Ghost bears witness to our praying?

Prayer is, I think, the language of heaven. A sage of old spake of prayer as thinking God's thoughts after Him. But in Spirit-born prayer, I believe we pray God's burden into and through our hearts. With God we share in prayer. Prayer is no magic transformation of words into heavenly language just because we close our eyes. Words are not prayer because we utter them on our knees, nor because we say them in the pulpit, nor yet because they are breathed within the confines of a church. Concerning our praying today, a phrase from Shakespeare often comes into my mind: "What do you read, my lord?" Polonius asked Hamlet. To this the melancholy man replied, "Words! Words! Words!" Likewise in prayer what do we so often say? Words! Words! Words! We can use words without praying, and we can pray without using words. We can also pray when words are used. But there is a language of the Spirit beyond words—groanings that cannot be articulated, that defy language, that are above language, that are beyond language, that are the yearnings of the heart of God committed to those who seek to know His will and to care for a lost world and feeble Church.

There is no stagnation in the Holy Ghost, for "holy men of God spake *as they were moved by the*

Holy Ghost." The Spirit "moves." In the beginning when this old world was like a slab of ice—lifeless and locked in the black womb of the universe—the Spirit moved and the earth came forth. Years later the Spirit "moved" over the matrix of the Virgin Mary and brought the Son into being. When that Son was laid dead in the tomb, the Spirit came and wrought the mighty resurrection. In the upper room the Spirit brooded over the men; then the world felt the impact of that Spirit operation. The mighty Roman Empire knew Spirit-filled men were around. The temple crowd, in their great authority, knew the Spirit had come on the upper-room men. Even now, the world still feels the tremor from that Spirit-baptized group who waited for the promise of the Father. The Spirit *moved* on those upper-room men. They in turn *moved* out to the lost multitudes. These multitudes were in turn *moved* upon by the Holy Ghost's moving through men.

Has the blessed Spirit toned down His operations? With reverence we ask, "Did God close down His production lines after the Spirit had come upon Wesley, upon Finney, and such men? Were those leaders spiritual freaks? Were they oddities of grace, eccentrics who were a little 'off' in their spiritual operations?" These days we are spiritually so *sub*normal that to be just normal (according to the New Testament pattern) seems to make us *ab*normal.

Despite the psychologists (the Freud and Jung followers of the gleaming star of human knowledge), we still have to admit that the human body is a mystery, and that the human mind is complicated and ambiguous; and so there are depths in man that

only the Spirit knows (I Cor. 2:11). Yet if the Holy
Spirit is power, we need to learn how to operate the
throttle. And if the Holy Spirit is a Person (and He is),
then we really need to learn how to let Him operate us.
I admit to being resentful when some soul, uninstructed
in the Spirit, suddenly closes a prayer meeting that
very obviously the Spirit has in control. How can
shrinking flesh be so stupid? We cannot turn the
Holy Spirit on and off with the lights of the sanctuary.
If President Kennedy invited us to hear him give a
speech, would we dare leave his presence on any given
impulse? We often presume upon Christ's promise
connected with "two or three gathered together in [His]
name" because *if* we were gathered "in His name,"
then we would be gathered *by* His Spirit. I feel deeply
that we trifle with the Holy Ghost even in prayer.
What a trivial round of petitions we get in the average
prayer meeting!

In prayer we need *holy* men, for holy men are
bold, reaching out in the Spirit and feeling the tug of
divine yearnings. Like their Master, holy men also
know strong crying and tears. Would to God our
Bible schools would give a special period each year
to training men in prayer.

Satan fears prayer and offsets it at every angle.
At every opportunity he stalls the impulse to take part
in it, for he has felt the smart of men who pray in
the Holy Ghost. Again and again hell has shuddered
because of the onslaughts of men who have taken
the kingdom of heaven by violence. In the book of
Acts we read that demons cried, "Jesus I know and
Paul I know." Because Paul knew how to pray in the

Holy Ghost, hell rocked in fury. Bloody Mary is said to have feared the prayers of John Knox more than the tramping feet of armies. Has the devil less intelligence than that queen? Ah brethren, in this kind of praying most of us feel like worms (Isa. 41:14)—a blessed experience if it is not mock humility.

Years ago in Dundee, Scotland, I stood reverently and read the great inscription on the cornerstone of the Church of St. Peter, where Robert Murray Mc-Cheyne used to minister. McCheyne knew Hebrew well enough to converse with learned European Jews. His scholarly tastes gave him appetite for finer poets of the Greek classics. He kept his diary from prying eyes by writing in Latin. He was no mean musician. As a hymn writer, his great hymns ("Jehovah Tsid-kenu" and "When This Passing World Is Done") gave him a place with the immortals. He also painted fine pictures. But Robert Murray McCheyne excelled in a greater art than any of these or all of them combined, for McCheyne is remembered as a man of prayer. Churches larger than his offered a rich price tag for his ministry, but with grace he refused them all. He was contented with his lot because no church could offer him more time for prayer. "How real God is!" he once said to himself. "God is the only person I can talk to."

After this saintly pastor's death, a visitor went to see the great church. The sexton showed him around. Some of McCheyne's books were still there. "Sit down here," said the canny sexton, leading the young visitor to the chair where McCheyne used to sit. "Now put your elbows on the table." The visitor obeyed. "Now put your face in your hands." The visitor again obeyed. *"Now let the tears flow. That* was the way Mr. Mc-Cheyne used to do!"

Then the amazed visitor was led into the very pulpit where the impassioned McCheyne had once poured out his soul to God and poured out God's message to the people. "Put your elbows on the pulpit," instructed the old sexton. The elbows were put in place. "Put your face in your hands." The young man obeyed. *"Now let the tears flow. That* was the way Mr. Mc-Cheyne used to do!"

To be much *for* God, we must be much *with* God. Jesus, that lone figure fasting in the wilderness, knew strong crying, along with tears. Can one be moved with compassion and not know tears? Jeremiah was a sobbing saint. Jesus wept! So did Paul. So did John. Mr. Bounds says, "There are tears that are only the surface slush on the iceberg." (Such tears are bursts of emotion.) But there *are* tears that are as blood from the heart.

Oh brethren in the ministry, I pray that you and I might covet something of this holy art of intercession. As I see it, there are two things for a minister to do— pray and preach. The mighty men of the early Church gave themselves to prayer and the Word and left to the elders the serving of tables and visiting of the sick. Even so, the elders were men of faith and of the Holy Ghost. Yet in our day the qualifications for an elder seem to be that he has a bit more cash than other members. How we need Bible elders as well as Bible preachers! Not long ago I went to speak at a church where a fine man had resigned as an elder. "I am not ruling my house as I should," he said, "and therefore I am Biblically disqualified from holding that office." Honest soul!

The early Church prayed; every revival church has prayed; every participant in revival prayer has known travail. Though there are some tearful intercessors behind the scenes, I grant you that to our modern Christianity, praying is foreign.

At a Bible conference in England, I met a fine-built man who was laboring deep in the bowels of the earth as a coal miner. In a quiet talk he told me that he knew a little about a burden for revival. Because of this prayer burden, he said that for twenty one days he had labored in the oppressive heat of the coal mine without food and with as little water as possible. From that prayer period he emerged spiritually renewed and without physical harm. He had learned to pray in the Holy Ghost.

O my Saviour, I say to Thee again with more insistence than ever: Teach me to pray; implant in me all the dispositions needful for the prayer of the Holy Spirit. Make me humble, simple and docile; may I do all that is in my own power to become so. Of what use is my prayer if the Holy Spirit does not pray with me? Come, Holy Spirit, come to dwell and work within me! Take possession of my understanding and of my will; govern my actions not only at the moment of prayer but at every moment. I cannot glorify God nor sanctify myself save by Thee.

—Jean-Nicolas Grou (1750)

CHAPTER SIX

PRAYERLESSNESS IS SIN

A bankrupt who had a millstone of debts around his neck would not delay long in using blank checks signed by a millionaire and specially donated to him for his distress. Why then do we Christians delay in using the "exceeding great and precious promises" which have already been signed by the Pierced Hand? Do we doubt our Lord's ability to answer, and are we afraid of over-reaching in prayer in order to implement the fulfillment of our petition? Is it that we shrink from prayer because God may demand the use of *our* flesh as substance even as He did Hannah's?

We sing:

"Channels only, blessed Master,
But with all Thy wondrous pow'r
Flowing *through us* Thou canst *use us*
Ev'ry day and ev'ry hour."

But does it make sense to sing these words and then shrink from the expenditure of God's operation through *our* human attributes to answer our own requests? If God were to commission angels to serve

63

Him down here, heaven would be empty of angels in five minutes. But God wants men! He wants obedient men, broken men, weeping men, resolute men— men strong in courage, men strong in will, men of ability, men of durability.

Prayer is taxing. Prayer is exacting. Prayer means enduring. Prayer means denying self, a daily dying by choice. But someone says, "There's nothing wrong in going fishing for a couple of hours." Maybe not if you are prayed up. Yet there is something wrong when we go fishing or do some other thing without the Spirit's leading. It is wrong when instead of praying we do things just to please others. There cannot be two operators of the Christian's life. We are either Spirit led in everything or self led.

We may call prayerlessness neglect, or lack of spiritual appetite, or loss of vision. But that which matters is what God calls it. In I Samuel 12:23 God calls prayerlessness sin: "God forbid that I should *sin* against the Lord in ceasing to pray for you." Prayerlessness is disobedience, for God's command is that men ought always to pray and not to faint. To be prayerless is to fail God, for He says, "Ask of me." *Prayerlessness is sin.*

Good seed sown on bad ground will produce an indifferent harvest; good preaching on ground ill-prepared by prayer is an abortive thing. In a church that had grown much during its present ministry, a pastor's wife said to me, "If this church has grown so much with so little praying, what would it have yielded with much praying?" That question we might ask today in a thousand churches throughout the nation.

The man behind the pulpit must have a prayer life. "A holy man," Robert Murray McCheyne used to say, "is a fearful weapon in the hands of a holy God." With prayer behind him, he can carry all before him. Prayer links man's impotence to God's omnipotence. Prayer swings us out of the natural into the supernatural. Prayer turns our stony words into' bread because He who turned water into wine still longs through the preaching of the Word to impart nourishment to heaven's pilgrims.

In our immediate setup, the minister is often the one through whom spiritual wealth is given to the church or withheld from it. Again this denotes the fearful responsibility of the preacher. No office on earth carries more peril with it than that of the ministry of the Word. To preach just because the Sabbath comes around is wrong; to preach just to fill in an hour, or less, is wrong; to preach for the sake of preaching is evil. Preaching does have perils.

I well remember Jock Purves saying that he felt one of the greatest things John Knox ever did was to dismiss an audience with just the benediction. He preached no sermon at all because he had no word from the Lord for the people. Most of us preachers would have warmed up an old sermon, arguing, "We are preaching truth," and covered our argument with the verse, "The truth shall make you free."

When preachers lack unction, no one is fooled. That preacher has not gone far who, after he has ministered the Word, needs the back slap of friends or the stimulant of others' flattery in order to "feel

good." The preacher who is elated over human praise
for his preaching will sink under human criticism.
This proves that he is walking in the flesh. A pastor
can be inexpressibly happy after preaching a word
from heaven even if his congregation storms at him.
The man who has gotten God's word in the prayer
closet neither seeks nor expects encouragement from
men for the delivery of that word. He is (or should
be) the servant of the Lord and not the tool of. men.
The Spirit himself bears witness of the approval. God
says, "Not with eyeservice, as menpleasers; but . . .
doing the will of God from the heart."

> "Men heed thee, love thee, praise thee not.
> The Master praises! What are men?"

There is a magnificent passage for believers: "If
children, then *heirs* [wonderful]; *heirs of God* [more
wonderful still]; and *joint-heirs with Jesus Christ*
[most wonderful of all]." Oh, the wealth of God, but
the poverty of the Church! What power God has, but
what patent poverty the Church demonstrates! We
must rediscover the power in the name of Jesus.
Heaven's powerhouse is overcharged with dynamic,
but there is a short circuit here in the church. *Is it in
me?*

It is when men bow the knee and call upon God that in a sense they become as mighty as the Almighty. Do not misunderstand me. I am not being irreverent. I am only saying what He says in His holy Word: "Call unto me, and I will answer thee, and shew unto thee great and mighty things, which thou knowest not." "You pray," says the Almighty God, "and I will work. If you ask anything in My name, I will do it. Call upon me in the day of trouble: I will deliver thee, and thou shalt glorify me." —J. F. Huegel

CHAPTER SEVEN

"THE PROMISE IS TO YOU"

Millenniums ago the Psalmist wrote, "He that goeth forth and weepeth, bearing precious seed, shall doubtless come again with rejoicing, bringing his sheaves with him."

"He that goeth forth and weepeth. . . ." We shall stop right there. Behind the picture in this verse lies a local truth. One old interpretation of it, I am told, is that the sowing of the seed was really a sacrifice. While the husband would be sowing, his tearful wife would be following him through the field and begging him not to sow, or else to sow sparingly. Why? Because they had very little seed to last them until next harvest time. The going forth and sowing meant they would feel the pinch. Do we hesitate today at God's price tag for intercessory prayer, or at the prospect of His putting upon us an unwanted burden? Is this why we falter in prayer?

I beg permission to be repetitious here, for I have said before that if we were half as spiritual as we think we are, we would be going to church these days as with sackcloth on our bodies and a handful of furnace ashes to anoint our unworthy heads. Surely the Lord's anger against man's rebellion cannot hold out much longer. With almost a blatant indifference we "hold the truth" in God. Where is the going forth *and weeping?* Where, oh where are the tears over this lust-bound age of sinners, over the lost millions in heathen lands, and over the cultured pagans on our own doorsteps? We would like to weep, but we are too busy and at the moment have too much of the dust of Time in our eyes to get the tears of Eternity moving. Yet if we are ever going to sow the seed of effective praying, the tears are going to flow.

Notice the next phrase of the promise: "Bearing precious seed." The seed is precious—costly. However, is it not true that from many of our lives God gets the scraps? We pray to Him *if* we are not too tired; we go to prayer meeting *if* it is not raining; we pray for the heathen *if* we are constantly being jabbed by prayer circulars. Shall we render unto the Lord that which costs us nothing? We will have to sacrifice precious things in our lives if we are going to learn the great art of intercession. We are to offer to God *sacrifices* of righteousness (Psa. 4:5), and one such sacrifice is named—"a broken spirit: a broken... heart, O God, thou wilt not despise" (Psa. 51:17). There are unbroken seekers after God these days because there are unbroken preachers—preachers unbroken in prayer. We preachers can have a "whole" prayer life only at the cost of breaking something else and something precious. Many have told the writer that they covet a real prayer life, but the pressure of business makes it almost impossible.

The first line of Elisha Hoffman's well-known song echoes Paul's strong words in Galatians 5:24: "They that are Christ's *have crucified... the affections.*"

Have thine affections been nailed to the cross?
Is thy heart right with God?
Dost thou count all things for Jesus but dross?
Is thy heart right with God?

Crucifixion of the flesh falls heavily on young folk. They are made for love and are in the romantic part of life. Yet affections can play havoc with devotional life. I believe it is but simple logic to say that a Christian is backslidden if he spends more time with a member of the opposite sex than he does in prayer and in the Word. Are the affections not uncrucified if the *human* life is paramount?

Satan wages relentless warfare against the souls of men. The more ground young people yield to God the more bitter the enemy's fight to recontrol that area. Then, too, love is blind. Humorous as it may seem, it is nevertheless true that nothing puts a blind spot on the eye like human love. Love hides a multitude of sins and also often blinds us to the immense possibilities that self-denial makes in this realm. Many young people have offered tearful prayers too late—not necessarily because they married the wrong person, but because they married too soon. In a short time they were saddled with children and often with debt, so that they were unduly burdened and also hindered in Christian service.

Crucifying of the natural affections is also for the married folk. That rugged Christian warrior, C. T.

Studd, did not see his wife for almost thirteen years, except for a two-week period. After preaching to outcasts, Mrs. William Booth tramped through the wet streets of London many a night. (She frequently had painful walking, too, for children were born fairly often.) I well remember Mrs. Rees Howells of the Bible School of Wales telling me that her husband prayed for twelve hours a day for eleven months about a major issue in his life and in the life of the Wales Bible School. There is often a crucifixion of one's affections when the call comes for an extended fast or for a retreat for prayer. When friends or relatives are coming, and one has to choose the spiritual instead of the carnal, the same demand is made. The price tag for effective prayer differs for every one of us, but the fact remains that a true Spirit-praying person will have much of his domestic life shattered.

On the human level, we each tread our path to the skies alone. Notice the text: *"He"*—not they, and not we—"that goeth forth." The subject is singular. Alone he goeth weeping, bearing seed. There are no mass production lines in grace. This is where the test of spiritual stamina comes in. What is my breaking point? With how much dare the Lord challenge me?

Today when rough land is being broken up, a farmer often drives his horses or tractor alone. The weather is inclement, the pace slow, the going difficult, but visualizing the harvest time, he holds on—alone. Yet when that time comes, he calls in many to gather in the precious grain. Thus it is in the spiritual world: a few break up the fallow ground in hearts and sow it with precious seed, but an army may be needed to gather the God-blessed results.

The phrase "bearing precious seed" suggests a back bent under a load of grain. In connection with prayer, it suggests a heart bent and then broken—bowed and shattered under today's almost hopeless world situation. In connection with prayer it may also mean bearing scorn. Many, even though they are Christians, think lightly of prayer. They look askance at those who know extended periods of prayer.

There must also be a bearing of the load. There may be those entreating us not to live at such a pace, not to be too severe upon ourselves. The flesh will squeal for more attention. A loved one may smart us that we are neglecting him. But the seed is the Word. It must be sown in our hearts and then allowed to fructify. Then we can bear it to others. Oh for a generation of Christians that are grown-up in Christ. "Be no longer children," says Paul. Children cannot bear their kind. Maturity alone brings powers of reproduction. This is the way, too, in the Christian life. God is looking for "a man" to stand in the gap. This position cannot be entrusted to the immature, the spiritually under-developed, but to men. Paul says, "When I became a man, I put away childish things." Many of us have many things to cast *off* before the Lord will put *on* us anything like a real prayer burden.

Recently we were in meetings with a gospel team. During the Spirit-anointed time, a fine man returned to the Lord after years of wandering and failure. His recovery was full and complete, a miracle of grace.

I think those present will not forget this brother's prayer for some time. While praying, he broke into tears and was unable to finish, for the Lord had revealed to him something of *the lostness of men*. That burden for lost men continued. This lostness must be borne until the Lord removes it, if He chooses and in His good pleasure.

"Shall doubtless come again." The whole result of this sowing effort swings on that word "doubtless." Obey the laws God has set for a harvest—the law of sowing, the law of weeping, and the law of bearing— and *doubtless* we shall come again—"with rejoicing." Then mourning will be turned into dancing, and the garment of praise will displace the spirit of heaviness. The old promise still stands: "He that goeth forth *and weepeth*, bearing precious seed, shall doubtless come again with rejoicing, bringing his sheaves with him." The word of the Lord endureth forever: Go weeping! Come rejoicing!

How wilt thou get a word from God if thou do not seek it? And how canst thou seek it but by earnest prayer? If otherwise, thou mayest get something that is the product of thy empty head to mumble over before the people, and spend a little time with them in the church. But O, it is a miserable preaching where the preacher can say, "Thus say I unto you, but no more"; and cannot say, "Thus saith the Lord."
—Thomas Boston of Simprin (1699)

CHAPTER EIGHT

THE PREACHER AT PRAYER

Let old Master Bounds give us a lead into the subject of the preacher at prayer. In *Prayer and Praying*, Bounds says this: "He who would teach the people to pray must first himself be given to prayer. He who urges prayer on others must first tread the path of prayer himself. Just in proportion as preachers pray will they be disposed to urge prayer upon those to whom they preach; moreover, just in proportion as preachers pray will they be fitted to preach on prayer." If that course of reasoning be true, would it be legitimate to draw the conclusion that the reason there is so little preaching on prayer in these modern times is that preachers are not praying men? Quarrel with this master in Israel if you like, but I for one say amen to his shattering indictment.

The preacher *must* pray. It is not that he *can* pray or that he *could* pray but that he *must* pray if he intends to have a spiritual church. There is no other way to power but by prayer. Hidden prayer is like heat smoldering in the bowels of the earth far beneath the still cone of a volcano. Though to the eye there

77

may be years of inactivity, sooner or later there will
be an explosion. So it is with prayer in the Spirit.
It never dies. There may be a long birth pain in the
Spirit, but birth there will be. The Holy Spirit is
looking for a body to indwell.

What a millstone the preacher has around his neck
if he is not a praying man! Men misuse the preacher,
demons taunt him, the flesh fails him, courage waxes
and wanes in him, congregations ebb and flow before
him, props fall beneath him, some forsake him, others
disown him. How can a mere mortal take it all if he
is not a praying man? Moreover, when a minister
has to bow out, and when, like John the Baptist,
he is succeeded and then exiled—how can he step
aside unless there remains for him a greater hidden
ministry than his previous public ministry? An
eminent actress once declared that she never wanted
the beauty of another great actress "because,"
she said, "I could never take it when the beauty
began to fade." This much is sure, and note it well:
A praying preacher is never envious of another man
whose pulpit mastery exceeds his own. He glories that
another can explain the way of the Lord more per-
fectly and glue the ears of a shifty congregation to
the Word of the living God.

What dearth in pulpit praying there is these days!
Recently I met a man who had been on a tour of
Europe and had heard many preachers. Almost the last
one he heard was my good friend, Dr. Martyn Lloyd-
Jones of Buckingham Gate Chapel, London (the church
renowned for the great ministry of Dr. Campbell Morgan). "Dr. Martyn Lloyd-Jones amazed me," said the

friend. "He prayed in the pulpit for almost fifteen minutes, and what a range he covered!" Another preacher whose prayers were not mere flights of oratory was Dr. Joseph Parker. Many of his prayers are recorded before the chapters in *The People's Bible* (now printed in the U.S.A. as *Preaching Through the Bible*).

A pastoral prayer sticks in the mind like nothing else except the word of the Lord. Often it is a source of soul balm to the listeners. In it the stillness of eternity can creep down. I can still hear the echo in my own heart of the prayers of men like Samuel Chadwick, Joseph Brice. David Matthews, Dr. Dinsdale Young of Westminster, and Dr. Luke Wiseman the worthy occupant of John Wesley's pulpit in the City Road, London. How could any of us forget the praying of W. E. Sangster? What tenderness! I can "feel" something when I recall the prayers of Dr. Martin Niemoeller and of others. I shall never forget the first time I had prayer with Dr. Paul Rees. One certain phrase he used still lingers fragrantly.

Another memorable prayer that has stuck with me is that of a nurse. Her name was Molly McPherson. (I can still "hear" that prayer after more than a decade.) She was at the same hospital as another nurse, who is now my wife. Molly came to the midweek prayer meeting after a heavy day of foot-slogging on a tiring ward and prayed like this: "Lord. I don't want to carry burdens others make for me, nor burdens the devil makes for me, nor burdens the church wants to put on me. nor burdens from myself. But I do want to carry the burdens *You* make for me." That to me is a classic in prayer. I have told of it all over the world, and people have thanked me for the prayer that Molly made.

There is a story told of Rubinstein (often attributed to other great artists too). The maestro said, "If I miss my piano practice one day, I know it; if I miss practicing two days, my friends know it; if I miss these exercises three days, the world knows it." Thus we preachers can trick people (not always intentionally) with slipshod study, but we cannot trick them with slipshod praying. The church both knows and feels if we miss our secret prayer.

Charles Haddon Spurgeon once went to a special meeting and was shown the program for the great rally: "Mr. —— would lead the meeting; Brother —— would pray; Mr. —— would read the Scriptures; another would appeal for the offering; a selected one would sing; and Mr. Spurgeon would preach. Each participant, it was explained, should take only one part. Said the famed Spurgeon, "If there is only one thing that I may do tonight, I want to offer the prayer." Wise man! We preachers must teach prayer; if we do not, we are unfaithful ministers of the New Testament. But we must do more than teach prayer; we must teach it by practicing it.

Here is a delicious word from Hubert Brooke about John Fletcher of Madeley. Fletcher, a great teacher of two centuries ago, was one of Wesley's fellow-workers and a man of most saintly character, who used to teach the young theological students. Whenever he spoke on one of the great topics of the Word of

God (such as the fullness of God's Holy Spirit or the power and blessing God meant His people to have), he would close his lecture and say, "That is the theory; now will those who want the practice come along to my room." Again and again they closed their books and went away to Fletcher's room where the one hour's theory would be followed by one or two hours of practice in prayer.

I am ever grateful that Samuel Chadwick wrote *The Path of Prayer;* I am more grateful to have heard him speak on prayer; I am grateful most of all because he prayed. Great theologian he was. Great pulpit master he became. Yet, like his Master, he was pre-eminently a man of prayer.

We hear a great deal these days about pulpit personalities. P. T. Forsyth anticipated this. Hear him: "No man has any right in the pulpit by virtue of his personality or manhood in itself, but only in the sacramental value of his personality for his message. The church does not live by its preachers but by its Word." Further he says, "Does anyone seriously doubt that the classic beauty of the face of Alexander Whyte, the piercing eagle eye and sharp-cut profile of Alexander Maclaren, the angelic transparency of the countenance of the youthful R. J. Campbell had much to do with the pulpit success of their possessors?" It is true that these characterstics might have added a little spice to the ministry of these pulpit giants, but again I appeal to Samuel Chadwick. Unlike Alexander Whyte, Chadwick was what the Americans call "homely." What a bulbous nose! (Of this he often made fun.) What narrow shoulders! What an oversized head for so small a frame! Chadwick was no Adonis. Dr. Parker of City Temple, London, had a leonine head, but that in itself did not make him magnetic. The truth is that a man fills a pulpit with more than physical attributes.

It is my considered opinion that in preparation for the ministry, our Bible schools need a major revolution in their teaching. In almost every science, this is the day for the specialist. I know a Christian doctor with a long record of faithful work in his line who had to leave a certain hospital because he would not take an extension course in order to qualify as a specialist. His quarter century of vast experience in the medical field as well as his surgery experience is looked down upon by "the new boys" in the hospital who know only textbook surgery. I am sure we need specialists in the pulpit. It is my solemn conviction that if a man is a preacher, he can be nothing else. (Paul mentions one deviation in his ministry.) Many pulpit men today are itching for money, and many preachers have to do secular work on the side because they need more money for things they do not need. By what twist of teaching can we claim we are following the apostolic method these days? The preaching men of the early church would not serve tables. Their slogan was this: "You deacons ought to look after the widows, feed the hungry, care for the orphans; we apostles will give ourselves to prayer (not golf) and the Word of God." (Preachers today have too many irons in their bags.) Who ever knew a preacher that prayed and studied and also failed? The criterion of success for the minister is certainly not the size of his audience, but whether through that ministry the Spirit is producing saints.

I would appeal for more preparation for the pulpit, particularly the preparation of prayer. Dr. Campbell Morgan used to say that he despised the Saturday night preacher—the man who, a day before he has to preach, is as empty as the proverbial drum. To escape from complete embarrassment, he snatches "dead men's brains" and, stringing a few thoughts together from other men's hearts, offers "a sermon." It might scrape through as a sermon, but I am adamant here in saying that it certainly is not a message. One old saint of bygone years used to say that the minister should have one day to prepare his sermon and then have Saturday to prepare himself to deliver the prepared sermon. Costly advice! But I guarantee there will be a new ministry, plus a new congregation, for any man who will take it. A distinguished pulpiteer of our own day says to the preachers, "Brethren, by our preaching we are not producing saints." How right he is!

In my judgment there are four ways a preacher can fill a church: by preaching, by organizing, by visiting people, by revival. The first man who fills his church is the preacher. I was thrilled to learn that Dr. Helmut Thielicke, a professor in the University of Hamburg, West Germany, is packing four thousand people into his church on a Sunday morning with nothing to attract but the Bible; on Sunday night there is the same number, and on Wednesday night almost another four thousand crowd into the church to hear a repeat of the Sunday night sermon. That's preaching! Watch the crowd, too, as they listen to the meaty expositions of Dr. Martyn Lloyd-Jones. Or who ever

came from the sanctuary unfed or unblest or unmoved
after hearing Dr. A. W. Tozer? Let Paul Rees' name
be in the newspaper as a speaker in this city where
I write (Minneapolis), and you will need to rush for
a seat. These are men with a message, men who have
given themselves to prayer and the Word of God.

The next man who fills his church is the organizer.
He may bring in converted cowboys and pulpit show-
men, but he gets the crowd. The third method for
church filling is a visiting church, by which I mean
a church group who takes upon itself in the name
of the Lord to visit the sick, the lost, the needy. They
too succeed. The last method of filling a church is
that of revival—I mean a limited revival. Wonders will
happen if the pastor is a praying man and has a praying people. But prayer cannot be rushed, for God cannot
be rushed. Wesley used to say to his ministers, "You
have only one thing to do—win souls." Measured by
this yardstick, many ministers would be a failure.

For a week I had the joy of ministering to a fine
audience at a yearly conference. My soloist, Anton
Marco, told me of an interesting experience when
he was taking the principal basso part in the opera
Pagliacci. Entering the Grand Opera House in the
late afternon, Anton took the stage to test the accous-
tical properties of the great hall. Next he went back-
stage to be familiar with his dressing room. Outside
dressing room No. 1 was a light. Thinking only a
cleaner might be there, Anton entered but then stopped
short. There, fully-robed, bearded, and stacked with
grease paint was Giovanni Martinelli, absorbed in
his rehearsal. Anton watched and waited and then

introduced himself as the leading artist in the bass section.

"Do you not know, Martinelli, that there are still four more hours before the play opens?"

"Yes."

"You must have played this piece hundreds of times before."

"So I have," said Martinelli, "but I cannot afford one slip. I must know every move today."

No wonder Martinelli was a supreme artist, second only to Caruso in this part. I believe it is correct to say that the Opera Singers' Union demands that participants be in their rooms one and a half hours before the play opens. What if all the preachers formed a union and made a pledge to the Lord that they would be in their church offices an hour and a half before every preaching service in order to wash the busy world out of their hearts and get the touch of God on their souls for the immediate need? Brethren, how slovenly we are in matters pertaining to the kingdom of God! In our day, preachers need to pray more than preachers of any other time—but we probably pray less.

How true are the words of E. H. Bickersteth:

> All earthly things
> With earth will fade away;
> *Prayer grasps eternity.*
> Then pray, always pray!

No one is a firmer believer in the power of prayer than the devil; not that he practices it, but he suffers from it.   —*Guy H. King*

Being convinced that to be filled with the Holy Ghost was a better qualification for the ministry of the gospel than any classical learning (though that too may be useful in its place), after speaking a while in the schoolroom he [Fletcher] used frequently to say, "As many of you as are athirst for the fullness of the Spirit follow me to my room." On this, many of us instantly followed him and continued there till noon for two or three hours, praying for one another till we could bear to kneel no longer.
—*Thomas Benson speaking of John Fletcher*

CHAPTER NINE

PRAYING—LOVE IT OR LEAVE IT

Praying is something we love or we loathe. There is hardly a middle course. Reading one hundred expositions *about* prayer will never equal one vital experience *of* prayer. Men who pray want to pray. They do not argue about prayer; they do not just urge others to pray; they have no confidence in their prayers. They have happiness in being obedient and in calling on the name of the Lord. They have no faith in their faith. Their faith is in Jesus Christ.

Once again I say that at God's judgment bar we believers are going to be embarrassed, for as Dr. A. W. Tozer mentioned recently, "We are not only going to be judged for what we *have* done; we are going to be judged for what we *could* have done." That hurts. Oh what we *could* have done! Oh the sacrifice we *could* have made, the prayers we *could* have offered, the tears for the lost we *could* have shed, the souls we *could* have won to Christ! There are resources in God that we believers have never touched; there is wealth, spiritual wealth in God that we have never discovered;

there is power in God that we have left untapped—
all because we have been faithless and unbelieving.

When one comes to think of it, what a limited
doctrinal circle we tread in our Bible conferences
across the land! They remind one of the treadmill in
the museum at Cardiff, Wales. The setting is a dog
tied to a pole. There he treads, pushing against the
revolving platform but never getting anywhere. What
weary treading we Christians do! This is explained in
Paul's letter to Timothy: "ever learning and never able
to come to the knowledge of the truth." Woe unto treadmill Christians! Of all people, their need is to get into
the warm Gulf Stream of prayer.

Hazlitt tells in his writings of some who, though
able to translate a word into ten languages, still did
not know in any language what the thing itself signi-
fied. Similarly, would it not be true to say that many
"*say* prayers" while what the thing called prayer
really is, they do not know? Look at that devotee
before a shrine, or see that barefoot zealot tramping the
cold stone floor of a monastery, gazing starey-eyed
at a crucifix and mumbling as he speeds his beads
around. Do such know anything about true prayer?
According to the Word of God, we answer a resounding
No!

The prayer life is a lonely life. Samuel Chadwick
used to say, "True prayer is a lonely business." The
hypocrite requires an audience when he prays. He
wants to be heard when he wants to pray. He must
impress. True prayer requires sincerity. True prayer
requires purity. In heaven there will be no praying.

All the faith we exercise must be exercised here. All the praying must be done here, for heaven will not be a place to make up a pitiable backlog of unfinished praying.

To pray we must be Spirit-filled. Proofs of being filled with the Holy Spirit are offered by many. How they vary! *The first and foremost evidence of a baptism with the Holy Spirit is that one lives a holy life.* That is imperative, and all else fades in comparison. Immediately after the baptism of Jesus and the Spirit's descent upon Him at the Jordan, He was led of the Spirit into the wilderness and there tempted of the devil. But all the time of the conflict He was sustained by the Spirit and "returned in the power of the Spirit." This fact can be overlooked if we are not careful. None but God knows the full compass of what Jesus endured. It was of this wilderness experience, I think, that Paul later wrote: "[Jesus] offered up. . . strong crying and tears." (Some locate this strong crying in His Gethsemane experience, but I feel it also covers the forty days in the wilderness.) Even after those days of temptation, the devil was seeking to destroy the Son of God. But Jesus lived praying. After He came from the Jordan, He prayed; before choosing the twelve, He prayed all night. He loved praying. He loved His Father, and in prayer fellowshipped with Him. Jesus died praying. It is also written, "Our fellowship is *with* the Father." Is it? Or is our fellowship with each other *about* the Father? Or is it reading a book about another man's fellowship with the Father?

The Holy Spirit fills men—not "temples made with hands." All the stained-glass windows in the world, plus robed choirs and deep-throated organs, will not win the Holy Spirit to brood in a place brilliant and exotic to aesthetic taste. The Spirit dwells in a humble and contrite heart. Nevertheless when He comes in a personal Pentecost, He will also come, I am sure, as the Spirit of Prayer, for true praying is "in the Holy Ghost." The Holy Spirit as the Spirit of Power helpeth our infirmity in prayer. The Holy Spirit as the Spirit of Life ends our deadness in prayer. The Holy Spirit as the Spirit of Wisdom delivers us from ignorance in this holy art of prayer. The Holy Spirit as the Spirit of Fire delivers us from coldness in prayer. The Holy Spirit as the Spirit of Might comes to our aid in our weakness as we pray.

The Holy Spirit glorifies the Son; the Son glorified the Father. The Spirit-filled believer glorifies the Father and the Son and the Holy Ghost, because all of the persons in the Trinity operate so that our prayers may be fulfilled. Thus in prayer the Father grants the request through the Son, whom we implore through the Holy Spirit.

A notice board outside a church in England read, "Sunday next at 6:30 p.m., the preacher's subject will be 'The Unfinished Work of Christ.' " Before the appointed day, that minister was snowed under with a stack of letters, almost all of which related to his coming Sunday subject. Many letters were abusive; some charged him with ignorance; others thought he bordered on the blasphemous. Did he not know that the work of Christ was finished? Yes, he knew that on earth the work of Christ was finished, at least until the millennium. But he also knew the work of Jesus right now in heaven is to perfect the imperfect prayers of us mortals. He knew that the Lord of glory, triumphant over principalities and powers, and with the keys of death and of hell upon His girdle, "ever liveth to make intercession for us." He *ever* liveth. There is not the slightest chance that He will of His own choice abdicate His mighty throne. There is no possibility that He will have to step down because a greater than He takes over. His throne cannot be usurped. He has "overcome the sharpness of death and opened the kingdom of heaven to all believers." He wills that we be rich in grace, rich in power. The way to all this is through prayer. Most of us believe that Christ lived, that He had an amazing life, displaying power over all the power of the enemy, and that He is coming again. But we are losing much because we have forgotten that right *now* Christ is longing to share His power with His people. Christ said, "*I give unto you* power. . . over *all* the power of the enemy."

No man has ever yet desired to pray without ceasing, asked for that grace earnestly, and done everything suggested by God for its bestowal, without having obtained it. To suppose such a thing would be manifest absurdity. For who is it who gives you the desire? God, of course. Does He give it you in order that it may stay unfulfilled? That is impossible. He implants within you a desire for something with the intention of giving you that very thing; He will infallibly give it you if you ask for it in the right way; and He begs you, He urges you, He assists you to make the petition. —Jean-Nicolas Grou (1750)

CHAPTER TEN

THE MUST OF PRAYER

Isaac Watts wrote that fine stanza:

Great Prophet of my God,
My tongue would bless Thy name;
By Thee *the joyful news*
Of our salvation came,
The joyful news of sins forgiven,
Of hell subdued, and peace with heaven.

From this stirring poetry Samuel Chadwick, the President of Cliff College in England, chose the caption, *Joyful News*, for the school paper. As I sat reading this school paper in the third lecture hall at Cliff, I saw one day this arresting advertisement: "Any student may send twenty cents to the Rev. Tinsley Peet and have mailed to him three books on any Bible subject of his choice. No further cost involved." It seemed too good to be true. Off went my cash and a request for three books—one on praying, another on holiness, and the last on the Second Coming of Christ. Promptly my prize package with three choice books came back. I am eternally indebted to Preacher Peet, though I never saw him in person or heard him preach.

The top book in my packet had a flaming red cover and bright gold lettering which read, *Power Through Prayer* by E. M. Bounds. I resolved to go through this book immediately. But I did *not* do that. The book went through me! During lunch hour I stole away day by day and fed my inner man on the deep teaching of Mr. Bounds. To him, writing on the subject of prayer was not just a hobby. Prayer was his habit. Like his Master, Bounds rose early, often before dawn, for that soul-invigorating exercise of prayer. (I know of nine books that Bounds wrote, and seven of them were on prayer. I have just compiled the best of those books and put them into one volume.* Though it may seem ambitious, I desire that my little book may do for others what *Power Through Prayer* did for me.)

Revival is wrought by God through His Holy Spirit, who works in believers as the Spirit of Prayer. In that New Testament letter, the Epistle of Jude, which is small in size but great in message, we have what is probably the most succinct title for prayer in the whole of the sacred canon—"praying *in the Holy Ghost.*" There lies the secret of prayer.

To describe this generation we might well borrow the language of Isaiah and say: "Ah sinful nation, a people laden with iniquity, a seed of evildoers, children that are corrupters: they have forsaken the Lord, they have provoked the Holy One of Israel unto anger, they have gone away backward. . . . From the sole of the foot

*A Treasury of Prayer. Compiled by Leonard Ravenhill and published by Bethany Fellowship.

even unto the head there is no soundness in it; but
wounds, and bruises, and putrifying sores; they have
not been closed. . . . And the daughter of Zion is left. . .
as a lodge in a garden of cucumbers." Truly the
whole body of humanity is sick! To this terrible
situation, politicians and philosophies of men have
nothing to bring. The cause of the disease is spiritual.
God and His Church alone have the answer. Not a
few millionaires have thrown bushel baskets of money
into the church. Many of the elaborate buildings, with
crosses perched high upon them, adorn the highways,
and many are fulfillments of the prophecy, "Thou hast
a name that thou livest, and art dead." The church's
style is bold, the service cold. The places have finery
but no fire. They are super-modern but lack the
supernatural. The gas-filled highways are thronged with
folk who do not even turn their heads to see a church
any more, and who could not care less what we build.

I have heard it said that when bombs fall on
America, the folk will sprint helter-skelter for the
house of God. I once thought that too, and just at the
dawn of World War II was foolish enough even to
preach it in England. No, dear reader, more often
war hardens folk rather than softens them. In the last
war during air raids when bombs fell outside. some
men who were sheltering inside the old stone churches
gambled in the pews. This callous indifference to death,
this defiance of God with eternity but a heartbeat away,
strengthened my conviction that there is no substitute
for Holy Spirit conviction. "And he, when he is come,
will convict the world. . . of sin." Our immediate need
is for spiritual millionaires, men who can bring down

the wealth of the world above on this stricken church
age. It is my solemn conviction that the Lord put the
Church to groaning in this groaning creation (Rom.
8:26) that she might reach millions who would otherwise groan for aeons in a devil's hell.

In the blackest hour of Germany's insane battering
of England, when night after night whole landscapes
were blown away by heavy bombing, Winston Church-
ill stepped to the microphone and promised "blood
and sweat and tears." With his passionate spirit throb-
bing with love for what seemed to be the dying British
Empire, he called for renewed sacrifice and a further
tightening of the belts. Against the overwhelming fury
of the Huns, he appealed for a British bulldog grip
of the people, first upon themselves and then upon
their duty. He declared that when the tumult and
the shouting died, when the captains and Huns had
departed, future historians would say of the tiny island
of England and of its suffering people, "This was their
finest hour!"

With political leaders staring blindly today into
the crystal ball of human diplomacy, in the midst of
bankrupt humanistic philosophies, with hell opening
her mouth to swallow this generation, at this sad
juncture in the collapse of human dignity and the
blatant trading in sin—we who are Christ's have the
greatest opportunity of the ages to show forth the
power of the ascended Lord. Rise up, O men of God!
Let our battle song be that grand old song of Master
Isaac Watts:

When mountain walls confront thy way,
Why sit and weep? Arise and say,
"Be thou removed," and they shall be
By power of God cast in the sea.

All power on earth, all power in heaven,
To Christ, the Son of God, is given;
And from the throne He will endue,
And hindrances shall flee from you.

O'er all the power of fiend and man,
Say to the Lord, "I surely can."
Take from Him power on earth to tread
On serpent's sting, on dragon's head.

Whate're thou art, O mountain high,
Where'er thou art, in earth or sky,
Whene'er thou art, truth is the same,
"Be thou removed in Jesus' name!"

"Be thou removed!" Faith bids thee start
For yonder sea. Arise, depart;
I may, I can, I must, I will,
The purpose of my God fulfill.

May future historians say of us, "This was their finest
hour!"

Our knees, then, must bow to Him who thus walks in the midst of the golden candlesticks. Back we must go until the glorious Lord stands among us in all the majesty of His Holy Person, and until the Church, which is His by gift of the Father and by His own purchase, comes under His complete control. For too long our remiss ways have shut the gates against the heavenly breathing of His Holy Spirit. Back we must go until the Lord Jesus is gloriously unveiled so that the fragrance of His Holy Presence becomes again the saviourness and power of the Gospel. It is only our full return to the first state of the Church which will once again make our faith strong and vigorous, active and confident, and without fear and doubting. It is our return to what the early Christians were which will once more make our worship spiritual and our prayers and devotions fervent and zealous. Those mighty acts wrought by the apostles are possible again but only when those who love Him walk with Him in white. Therefore, He says, "Do the first works"— that is, do ye as the first Christians did.

—Author Unknown

CHAPTER ELEVEN

"THE FLESH IS WEAK"

As children we used to sing, "I often *say* my prayers. But do I ever pray?" Such truth is far beyond the grasp of a child's mind. Millions *say* prayers every day. To all such, prayer is just a superstitious formula; not to *say* a prayer before leaving home would not "feel safe." To them, prayer is a kind of insurance against calamity, a spiritual gambling, a game of chance, a religious lottery. (True prayer, of course, is actually none of these.)

To many others, prayer is a last resort instead of a first choice. For instance, a man once told about his brother who was so very ill that the church folk were praying for him. "Is he really as bad as that?" a neighbor asked. To yet others, prayer is a talisman or an escape mechanism, a good exercise for relieving mental strain. To some, prayer may simply be the outlet for a burden born of domestic pressure. Or prayer may be the habit of an incurable or uncured sinner who has been taught to "confess" and yet has not the least intention of forsaking sin. Like a sow that was washed, he returns to the mire and then keeps up his sinning and repenting cycle.

Prayer may also be treated as a spiritual wishing well or as a spiritual listening post when the mind is left open and a record of impressions is made of what is heard. Often prayer is looked upon as a spiritual gymnasium, a "must" if one is to keep fit spiritually. Much praying that I hear seems to be just giving God a shopping list on the basis of Paul's exhortation to "let your requests be made known unto the Lord."

Some of these suggested interpretations of prayer have an element of true prayer in them, but in the main are what I would call juvenile concepts of prayer. After much consideration (kind and honest, I trust) I am persuaded that most of us know less about this holy art of prayer than we know about our Bibles, even though we are aware of the shallowness of our Scripture knowledge.

It is strange but true that many of the noblest examples of prayer-burdened men were folk of human, physical frailty. Samuel Chadwick, the beloved and honored principal of Cliff College, England, was never robust at any time, yet he rose from the obscure task of a cotton mill operative to the eminence of president of the Methodist Church in England. On more than one occasion I well remember his saying. "Brethren, in my ministry I have given two-thirds of my time to Bible study and only one-third to prayer. But if I had my life to live over again, I would give two-thirds of my time to prayer and only one-third to Bible study." Dr. Chadwick was not saying that *our* talking to God in prayer is more important than *His* talking to us through His Word. I think I interpret his statement aright by saying Dr. Chadwick felt that in order to germinate in us, the seed of the Word needed a long time in prayer. My school teacher used to tell me that in one acorn there was a mighty oak. But didn't she know that in one acorn there is a forest? One *acorn* begets one oak; but one *oak* may beget a million acorns, which in turn would make a forest. Even so, just *one* seed-thought gathered from the Word of God may "spark a man off" in prayer for hours. That is why Chadwick wanted to change the ratios of his studying and praying.

I bless God for the discipline of Chadwick's majestic life. In our day, apart from the military and the monastery, there is little of discipline around. Most of us *want* to pray more; at times many of us have made vows to pray more. The Holy Spirit is willing and longing to bring to birth in the Spirit, *but* on our side we are weak and undisciplined. Our spirit is often willing—*but* weariness, or appetite, or the longing for fellowship or companionship, head us off from the prayer closet. The Spirit indeed is willing—*but* the flesh is weak. We want to learn the noble Spirit-initiated art of intercession—*but* there are friends coming. We want a closer walk with God (and prayer is the only way to get it)—*but* there are church activities calling. These are easier on the flesh than closeted prayer. The way we are going, we shall have our unfulfilled vows with us in our caskets!

The college which Samuel Chadwick enlarged in building and extended in influence was begun in a house in Rochdale, England, by Thomas and Mary Champness. They, too, were determined in prayer—so determined for souls and so ambitious to see Deity clothe men with power that they rose every morning and prayed from four to five o'clock. Their slogan was "Difficulties give way before determined men."

In later years Samuel Chadwick, though slow and frail (only in body), still prayed. I have seen his study light burning late at night, and yet early the next morning he was at prayer. In spirit, Samuel Chadwick was a flaming fire in the Holy Ghost until he died.

There is something mysterious about that four o'clock hour in the morning. John Wesley was a prayer habituate of the early hour. I know of the leader of a famous American Seminary who is past seventy years but who is at prayer by four in the morning, prays until six, and does physical exercises before breakfast. Master E. M. Bounds prayed at four a.m. too. Before me is his picture. At forty-five he looks like a man of eighty years. Here is a man spending and being spent for God. Of the Son of God, men said, "Thou art not yet fifty years of age." In point of fact, he was about thirty-three. But what was it that impressed them that He was older? Was this impression due to His wisdom? Or was it that His visage was "marred more than the sons of men" by reason of the extended hours spent in prayer?

Praying Payson of Portland, Oregon, was also slung on a frail human chassis. His glorious diary is open before me. Here is a man who after death was found with calloused knees. (Preachers should check here.) By his bedside were two grooves which his delicate knees had rubbed into the floor as he seesawed in travail for the lost. His diary records on December 19,

1807: "After a day of excessive fatigue, awoke twice, drenched in a profuse sweat, and concluded that my time was short." (He was then at the ripe old age of twenty-four years!) Yet for another twenty years, though saddled with weakness, he soared in the realms of prayer more than most men.

John Fletcher of Madeley, Shropshire, England, was the saint to whom the rolling drunks in the village doffed their hats and muttered, "There goes the man that loves our souls." Robert Southey said of Jean Guillaume de la Fléchere (Fletcher), "He was a man of rare talents and rarer virtue. No age or country has ever produced a man of more fervent piety and more perfect charity; no church has ever produced a more apostolic minister. He was a man of whom Methodism may well be proud, as the most able of its defenders, and one whom the Church of England may hold in remembrance as one of the most pious and excellent of her sons." (Southey was not usually so gushing with praise.)

"Fletcher was a saint," said Isaac Taylor, "as unearthly a being as could tread the earth at all!" Concerning this rare soul, the testimony of Robert Hall was this: "Fletcher is a seraph who burns with the ardour of divine love. Spurning the fetters of mortality, he almost habitually seems to have anticipated the rapture of the beatific vision." Dr. Dixon believed John Fletcher to be "the most holy man who has been upon the earth since the apostolic age."

Concerning Fletcher, Mr. Wesley said that on his part he could die and leave that thriving youngster, the Methodist Church, in the capable hands of the seraphic John Fletcher. But Wesley himself laid the mortal frame of Fletcher to rest and went on gathering spoils for the Master for another few years afterwards. When Mr. Wesley preached the funeral sermon for this mighty man, he declared, "Many exemplary men have I known, holy in heart and life, within many years. But one equal to him [Fletcher] I have not known, one so inwardly and outwardly devoted to God. So unimpeachable in character in every respect I have not found, either in Europe or America, and I scarce expect to find another such on this side of eternity. But the other-world air about this saintly man, the piety that drunks could see, the apostolic ministry that he conducted—these all were the results of his fervent prayer. Above all, Fletcher prayed." (I can quietly sigh and wistfully think that a tape recording of one of these prayers would be worth more than all the diamonds Kimberly ever raised.) Praying produced Fletcher's holy living; conversely, Fletcher's holy living produced prayer.

In northern Ireland, the name of W. P. Nicholson is greatly revered, and well it might be. I am told that the statute book of that Green Land has an entry something like this: "We expected revolution, but through W. P. Nicholson God sent revival." "W. P." took a dozen trips around the world, rubbed shoulders with the great and the famous, but "never lost the common touch." Thousands have been converted through his world-wide ministry. In his later years he reaped what he had sown—I mean in the realm of prayer—for pray he did at all times and in all circumstances. Sleep came to him in trickling doses in those years, but right there was where he triumphed. Propped up in his bed, W. P. prayed. That big heart of his thumped with holy passion right into his fourscore years and more. His flesh was weak, but, as is the secret of the saints, he mastered his body, and it became his servant, not his lord. (I hope and pray some husky young men will read this and begin the greatest ministry they can ever have—the ministry of intercession.) W. P. clearly demonstrated that a man who kneels before God will stand before men.

Again I say, no man is greater than his prayer life. Here we are either weighed in the balances and found wanting, or we are found with a "calm"—because the Spirit bears witness that we are living up to the light that we have in this matter.

There is a mysterious rejuvenation in prayer: "They that wait upon the Lord *shall renew their strength.*" (It does not say "put on weight.") This Scripture means, I believe, that what we pour out, God pours back—plus much more. I am glad we do not have to be a Hercules in order to pray. I am glad prayer is not geared just to the intellect. Prayer is *of* the Spirit of God *upon* the spirit of man. From musty cells like that of Bunyan's in Bedford, from the confines of the catacombs, from the steaming jungles, prayer has ascended and answers have come. In very limited bodies there have been, and still are, mighty spirits who have learned that when a hidden ministry is generated in prayer, it can do wonders.

There then is our list: Chadwick, Fletcher, Payson, Nicholson. Brainerd could be added, and so could John

Hyde, who was also an inveterate early riser. It was on quivering flesh that most of these men carried eternity within them. They were the weak things of the world that confounded the mighty. In the flesh they were weak; in God they were mighty to the pulling down of Satan's strongholds.

To strive in prayer means to struggle through those hindrances which would restrain or even prevent us entirely from continuing in persevering prayer. It means to be so watchful at all times that we can notice when we become slothful in prayer and that we go to the Spirit of prayer to have this remedied. In this struggle, too, the decisive factor is the Spirit of prayer.
—Dr. O. Hallesby

CHAPTER TWELVE

REVIVAL—WHAT SAITH THE SCRIPTURES?

A friend of mine once trounced an audience for the oft failures of us men to quote the Scriptures aright. He averred, "Our quotes are misquotes." How right he was! There and then he demonstrated this truth by misquoting the Sacred Book some half dozen times (e.g. Eve gave Adam an apple).

But are we not also guilty of misquoting the Royal Message in our ideas? Our thinking about the meaning of many of God's promises is not straight. At one time or another we have heard some soul begin this promise, "[Lord, Thou art] able to do exceeding abundantly above all that we ask or think," and there they stopped. But the sting of this truth is at the end of the verse. God is *able*, without a doubt, to do all that the first part of the verse implies—but read on. The promise is that God is able "... *according to the power that worketh in us*." Since something is obviously stopping the Spirit's inflow to us Christians, the same thing is stopping His outflow from us. With the Spirit's help we need to search for this hindrance. "God... searcheth the heart."

Another Scripture which comes in for pernicious and promiscuous use even more is Joel 2:28–32. Nothing seems to put a sagging prayer meeting back on its feet like the promise in these verses: "It shall come to pass afterward, that *I will pour out my spirit upon all flesh;* and your sons and your daughters shall prophesy, your old men shall dream dreams, your young men shall see visions: and also upon the servants and upon the handmaids *in those days will I pour out my spirit.*" Let us consider this passage at greater length.

In these turbulent days, some men use this Joel 2 promise as a sheet anchor for the soul, or else they hold it as a shining star of hope in the black sky of this moral midnight. But to isolate this text is unlawful, unscriptural, and therefore untrue. To do this is to use the hub of the wheel and reject the spokes. We must hold this text in its context or it is a pretext.

Of all the promises, this promise of revival to come "in *those* days" is obviously conditional. How choosy we Christians are! We take to ourselves the promises and leave alone all the curses. There is no Biblical warrant for us to take the sweet and leave the bitter. We are like a child whom I saw in a cafeteria. He grabbed three desserts and off he went. But his father soon altered that. Why do we Christians grab all the desserts? Yes, God has made promises *if* we do our part. For instance, the Bible says, "Open thy mouth wide, and I will fill it." But, my reader, just try opening your mouth wide for about three weeks. Lie in bed and wait. Will the promise be fulfilled that God will fill your mouth? Never!

An old Chinese proverb says that he who would take a thousand steps must take the first one. By the same token he who would claim Joel 2:28, 29 must start earlier in the chapter. Verse 12 would be a good starting point: "Therefore... saith the Lord, *turn ye even to me with all your heart*, and with fasting, and with weeping, and with mourning." In Joel's day pestilence and plague had destroyed the land (see Joel 1). Israel was a reproach among the heathen. God's command to them was to turn with all their hearts. They could have no other love. Thus in the minds of those who seek this heavenly operation of the Spirit, revival must be the first, the second, and the last thought. Revival must not be just a once-a-week concern in the midweek church prayer meeting. Would any girl become an opera singer by practicing once a week? No! She must give herself to singing.

Years back I was recovering from some slight illness from overwork and was taking a week's rest at Southport, England. In the house where I stayed were some of the world's top golfers, one of them Jimmy Adams. One night as we took dinner, a magnificent car drew up to the house and some wealthy people desired Jimmy Adams to go to dinner with them and visit with friends. Jimmy refused, saying, "I came here to play golf and must be on the links before breakfast. That means early practicing." I have never forgotten that man's zeal for his sport. Shall we be less sincere and less sacrificing for the glory of the Lord and the quickening of His Zion?

Here then are the ingredients of the first phase of our quest for outpoured blessing: "Turn ye even to me

with. . . fasting, with weeping, and with mourning"
(Joel 2:12). If on *our* part we do not obey these things,
how can we hold *God* to His part? Of course fasting
and weeping and mourning can be done in the flesh,
but we all know these avail nothing.

The prophet Joel's further exhortation is *"Rend
your heart, and not your garments,* and turn unto the
Lord your God" (vs. 13). Among the Orientals and
Jews there were and still are many ways of expressing
sorrow, indignation, and penitence. The Jews would
kneel in prayer, or fall in prostration, or stand lift-
ing up their hands, or hide their faces, or smite their
breasts, or, as the allusion is in Joel, rend their garments.

In Genesis 37:29 when Reuben returned and Joseph
was not in the pit, Reuben "rent his clothes." This
rending of the garments was again an outward sign of
inward grief, a sign of a broken heart. When the fearless
Elijah confronted Ahab, the king of Israel, with the
shattering prediction of the Lord: "Thus saith the
Lord, . . . dogs shall lick thy blood. . . ," Ahab "rent
his clothes, and put sackcloth upon his flesh, and
fasted, and lay in sackcloth and went softly. And the
word of the Lord came. . . saying, Because he [Ahab]
humbled himself before me, I will not bring the evil in
his days: but in his son's days will I bring the evil upon
his house." Here again from the Word of the Lord we
have fasting, sackcloth, and humiliation as a sign of
grief, and an operation that God favored. Years later,
when Jesus "held his peace," Caiaphas the high priest
was frustrated and infuriated. He "rent his clothes
saying, He has spoken blasphemy." The expression,

"rent his clothes," meant that the high priest had come to the end of himself.

If Reuben was heartbroken over the absence of his brother and rent his garments, and if Ahab put on sackcloth, ought not we, too, be distressed about the lost millions who wander into eternity without God and without hope? Should we not take up strong lamentation that the supernatural has departed from amongst the people of God? As I have said before, I repeat in order to challenge myself again: No longer do people go to the house of God to meet God; people go to the house of God just to hear a sermon about God.

The rending of the garments *could* drift into hypocritical formality. Behind the outward observance there could be no broken heart. Therefore comes the command. "Rend your hearts." We rend our hearts by godly consideration and self-examination; by the conviction of the Holy Spirit; by recognition of our failure to pray; by confessing that we have more appetite for material food than for spiritual; by acknowledging that we like the company of men more than the company of God; by abhorring ourselves because we love to play more than pray. It is possibly true to say that millions of our people who go to fundamental churches have never seen a preacher heartbroken, preaching with tears about the iniquity of the nations or the stonyheartedness of his people.

Our next instruction is a repeated one: *"Turn unto the Lord your God"* (vs. 13). They were admonished to turn *to* the Lord; so somewhere they had turned *from* Him. Why and where did they get moving in their own strength? When David the king grieved the Spirit, he was aware of it, but Samson *"wist not* that the Lord was departed from him." Are we like David, aware when we grieve the Spirit? Where did we begin to trust in the flesh, consciously or unconsciously? Rent hearts are not easily found amongst us these days. To most of us, fasting is out, tears are frowned upon, and mourning is associated with melancholia. How wise we are! But you will notice (and maybe notice it with pain) *we have no revival.* We are wondering why *God* does not move; He is wondering why *we* do not break! We have His exceeding great and precious promises and wonder why *He* does not oblige; He wonders why *we* do not obey! We wish *He* would bend low; He wishes *we* would break down.

The exhortation, then, is to turn unto the Lord. Somewhere we have turned from Him. We began in the Spirit but have ended up in the flesh; therefore we must turn to Him for forgiveness and cleansing from sin. When we grieve Him, He turns His face from us; so the Psalmist entreats earnestly, "Cause thy face to shine [upon us]; and we shall be saved." We must turn to God to receive compassion (without Him we have none) for the multitudes; we must turn to Him for power to pray; we must turn to Him for endurance to fast; we must turn to Him for vision; we must turn to Him for endurance to overcome principalities and powers.

The further exhortation is *"Blow the trumpet in Zion, sanctify a fast* [here's fasting again], *call a solemn assembly"* (vs. 15). This is no one-man effort. As one hundred and twenty tarried at Pentecost, the

Spirit descended because they were obedient. We today could at least try obedience. In our praying for revival there must be a single purpose, a single eye to His glory.

Look now at this God-given demand in Joel for an all-out effort in God's holy cause:

1. "Blow the trumpet in Zion,
2. sanctify a fast,
3. call a solemn assembly:
4. gather the people,
5. sanctify the congregation,
6. assemble the elders,
7. gather the children, and those that suck the breasts:
8. let the bridegroom go forth of his chamber, and the bride out of her closet.
9. Let the priests, the ministers of the Lord, weep.
10. Let them say, Spare Thy people, O Lord."

These might be called *the ten commandments for revival*. Observed by themselves, they are worthless and the book of Joel meaningless, but kept with holy fear and a passionate desire to see a divine visitation, these commands are the key to revival. The sounding of the trumpet belongs to the yesteryears as far as we Gentiles are concerned. Dean Stanley has this to say about it: "The harsh blast of the consecrated ram's horn called an assembly for an extraordinary fast. Not a soul was to be absent. Like the fiery cross, it convened old and young, men and women, mothers with infants at their breasts, the bridegroom and the bride on their bridal day. All were there stretched in front of the altar. The altar itself presented the dreariest of all sights—a hearth without its sacred fire,

a table spread without its sacred feast, the priestly
cast, instead of gathering as usual upon its steps and
its platform, were driven, as it were, to the further
space; they turned their backs to the dead altar and
laid prostrate, gazing toward the invisible Presence
within the sanctuary. Instead of the hymns and music
which, since the time of David, had entered into their
prayers, there was nothing heard but the passionate
sobs and the loud dissonant howls such as only an
eastern hierarchy could utter. Instead of the massive
white mantles which they usually presented, they
were wrapped in black goat-hair sackcloth, twisted
round them, not with the brilliant sashes of the
priestly attire but with a rough girdle of the same
texture. What they wore of their common dress was
rent asunder or cast off. With bare breasts they
waved their black drapery towards the temple, and
shrieked aloud, 'Spare thy people, O Lord!' " This
then is a vivid interpretation of the ancient ceremony
of sounding the ram's horn. This then was the meaning
of "blow the trumpet in Zion."

One of the great personal assets of Gideon was
that he had heard of the miraculous operations of
God in Israel's history. Thus when the angel of God
appeared to him telling him that he was a mighty
man and that God was with him, he seems to rap out
the answer immediately: "*If* God be with us, *where
be his miracles?*" What he had heard from his forebears
of the divine manifestation had left an unerasable
mark upon his memory.

Would it not be like that in Joel's day when this
solemn assembly was gathered? Here are aged people

mourning for the departed glory; here are little children gazing on weeping parents; here are the elders deeply moved at the judgments of God in the land; here is pathos because even the children are imperiled in this situation. Maybe even the tears of the children who were frightened would move upon their parents' hearts.

Right now the shadow of the atom bomb is over us. We are living in the most insecure period in human history. Recently in a Y.M.C.A. building in the States, someone posted a sign (a parody on the words of Abraham Lincoln that all men are *created* equal). The sign said, "If there is a third world war, all men will be *cremated* equal."

"Let the priests, and the ministers of the Lord, weep between the porch and the altar, and let them say. Spare thy people, O Lord, and give not thine heritage to reproach, that the heathen should rule over them: wherefore should they say among the people, Where is their God?" (Joel 2:17). In the time of this calamity that Joel speaks of, the priests, the ministers of the Lord, were to weep between the porch and the altar. This is a divine arrangement. This is a divine commandment. The priests were to meditate upon this calamity until their hearts were broken. They were to lead the way in repentance. They were to lead the way in tears. They were not to hide in a secret place but stand in the midst between the porch and the altar and cry aloud, "Spare thy people, O Lord. . . ." The priests were commanded both to weep and to pray.

It has been said, "Tears without prayers are vain."
In a time of calamity it might be right to say, "Prayers
without tears are vain." In a time of war we have
heard people pray with more concern about their skins
than their sins. The priestly cast no longer belongs
to a selected favored minority. The Lord hath made *us*
a kingdom of priests unto God. No honest Christian
evasively asks as did Cain, "Am I my brother's keeper?"
We believers have a built-in consciousness that we
are responsible to men and responsible, too, to God for
getting the message of redeeming grace to men.

Joel calls. What do we answer? In verses 18, 19, 20,
25, 28, 30, the manifold mercy of God is revealed.
Notice how positive this word is: "Then *will* the
Lord be jealous. . . . The Lord *will* answer. . .I *will*
send you corn. . .I *will* no more make you a reproach. . .I *will* remove far off from you the northern army, and *will* drive him into a land barren. . . .
I *will* restore to you the years that the locust hath
eaten. . . . I *will* pour out my Spirit upon all flesh. . . .
I *will* shew wonders in the heavens and in the
earth." What better investment could God give for
outpoured grief and for flowing tears over the departed
glory in the sanctuary than the offer of outpoured
blessing? He is faithful that promised. God still says,
"Prove me now."

*In the afternoon "God was with me of a truth."
Oh, it was blessed company indeed! God enabled me so
to agonize in prayer that I was quite wet with sweat,
though in the shade and the cool wind. My soul was
drawn out very much for the world; I grasped for
multitudes of souls. I think I had more enlargement for
sinners than for the children of God. though I felt as
if I could spend my life in cries for both.*

*I enjoyed great sweetness in communion with my
dear Saviour. I think I never in my life felt such an
entire weanedness from this world and so much resigned to God in everything. Oh. that I may always
live to God!* —David Brainerd (1740)

CHAPTER THIRTEEN

THERE WERE GIANTS IN THE CHURCH

America's spiritual history is replete with the names of famous intercessors. If its crime world has its Al Capone, its John Dillinger, and its Jesse James, then its spiritual heritage sparkles with names that will shine forever in the firmament of godliness—John Hyde, Edward McKendree Bounds, Edward Payson, David Brainerd, Charles Grandison Finney, and that quaint old character whom the squirrels fed, H. C. Bevington. New pages were written in American church history because of these stalwarts in that most noble art of intercession. These were the giants in the Church.

"John Hyde, the Apostle of Prayer," says Francis A. McGaw, "was reared in a home where Jesus was an abiding guest and where the family in that home breathed an atmosphere of prayer." John's father, Dr. Smith Harris Hyde, was himself a man of prayer.

In the world of music, Johann Strauss left his mark. He was appointed Kapellmeister to the first Burger regiment, and he composed for special events. But in musical circles, his son, Johann Strauss, Jr., came

121

along in haste, eclipsed his father, and was soon labeled
the "Waltz King." Wherever music is known, folk
hum or whistle or play his dreamy "Blue Danube."
In like manner, John Hyde surpassed his distinguished
father in the holy exercise of prayer and left India
an indenture in the praying records. He was in India
only nineteen years, but what glorious years! What
inspiration others got from this wrestling Jacob! Some
knew the more intimate seasons that Hyde had with
God. This holy John entered Gethsemane too.

God knew John Hyde; John Hyde knew God. Again
I say, there is all the difference in the world between
knowing the Word of God and knowing the God of
the Word. John Hyde's "homing instinct of the soul"
led him to the prayer closet. That was his habitat.
There he soared; there he listened; there he heard;
there he grew; there he wept; there he developed
spiritual muscle. Just as a man seeks the solitary place
to tell his love to the woman of his choice, so John
Hyde had a prayer harbor where his soul delighted
in the Lord and where the Lord delighted in him.
The only reason we have a record of John Hyde is
that in this art of prayer he was a master in our Israel.
Listening by John's door, men heard him weeping, even
as Jesus wept over Jerusalem and even as the Apostle
Paul wept for the stubborn sinners of his day. (No
Bible schools can teach us this art of tears.) Hyde
knew those "groanings which cannot be uttered." A
lady who often used to see him in India told me there
was always the air of another world about him. Yet
how he loved the souls of men! Few of my readers
have not read how John Hyde got to the place where
from leading *one* soul a day to Christ, he led *four*

souls a day to Him. He would stay on his face before God until the answer came clear. Even if he had to stay alone for as long as forty hours, yet he would not let God go until he knew the yea or nay of the Spirit in the matter for which he sought God.

Dr. J. Wilbur Chapman was once preaching in Hereford, England. For days there was a signal absence of power and conviction of sin. "But when John Hyde came there, God came to town," said Wilbur Chapman. God and Hyde walked together. (Amazing condescension of God!) As a result, when Chapman made the appeal on the first night after Hyde was in that town, fifty men came to Christ. Chapman begged Hyde, "Pray for me." Into a room these two men went; Hyde turned the key in the door, turned his face up to God, then turned the fountains of his great heart open. Chapman adds, "I felt the hot tears running down my face. I knew I was with God. With upturned face, down which the tears were streaming, John Hyde said two words: 'Oh God!' For five minutes at least, he was still again, and then when he knew he was talking with God, his arm went around my shoulder, and there came up from the depth of his heart such petitions for men as I had never before heard. I rose from my knees to know what real prayer was."

Down to his feeblest days, Hyde prayed. Hear him in a letter to his sister: "I am still in bed or in a wheel chair, getting a fine rest and doing a lot of the ministry of intercession." In the Lord's "book of remembrance" we shall see the mighty results of the prayer ministry that this lover of men's souls exercised.

Some men rebel against long intercessions with God, but what they cannot erase is that the record stands that men who prayed most accomplished most. Lasting prayers bring lasting revivals. Prayer does not condition God; prayer conditions us. Prayer does not win God to our view; it reveals God's view to us. Prayer is not merit, so that by withdrawing from the world we of necessity gain special favors of God. Prayer is not purchasing things from God. If you ask why we emphasize prayer so much and so often, we reply, "Because Jesus did so." The Gospel by Luke gives accounts of whole nights spent in prayer by the Saviour. Are we better than He?

In the records of revival in America, Charles Grandison Finney stands as a giant. If the report is true that he stood seven feet high, then physically he was a giant. There is no doubt that intellectually he was a giant. Finney was no fly-by-night evangelist. He could stay in some places for months and not be too worried when some sinner, maddened by what this Spirit-anointed man said, would stamp rudely out of the meeting, only to be followed in some cases by the whole congregation. But Finney had this pull over most of us: if he lost men by his strong preaching, he regained them by prayer. His own prayers? Maybe in part, but there were other factors.

As Moses had his Aaron and Hur, so Finney had his Father Clery and Father Nash. In Bolton, England, I had the inestimable privilege of being the assistant pastor to Arthur Fawcett (now Dr. Fawcett), a brilliant preacher in the Church of Scotland, who taught me to love books and told me of the old masters of the pulpit. I shall ever be grateful that he introduced me to the praying saints of the ages. While ministering with him, I met an old lady who told me a story about Charles Finney that has challenged me over the years. Finney went to Bolton to minister, but before he began, two men knocked on the door of her humble cottage, wanting lodgings. The poor woman looked amazed, for she had no extra accommodation. Finally, for about twenty-five cents a week, the two men—none other than Fathers Nash and Clery—rented a dark and damp cellar for the period of the Finney meetings (at least two weeks), and there in that self-chosen cell. those prayer partners battled the forces of darkness. With all due credit to Mr. Finney for what was done, it was the praying men who held the ropes. The tears they shed, the groans they uttered are written in the book of the chronicles of the things of God.

Praying Payson of Portland next engages our attention. Because this man had the highest quality of intercourse with God, he had extraordinary power with men. Most of us are but sparrows in prayer and flutter no higher than the lowest branches; but these "eagle" men soar into the heavenlies. None rose higher than Payson.

A lady once heard that the distinguished Lafayette was to be in Dr. Payson's church. and she hurried to the sanctuary. When Lafayette failed to enter. the lady was arrested by the unusual prayer of the pastor. Edward Payson. "May I have a copy of that prayer?" she asked. "The pastor did not write his prayer, and the prayer passed on the wind and into the heavenlies," was the reply. Astonishment took hold of the lady, and the record says that she was "filled with admiration of the intercessory part of the exercises as differing from all that she had ever heard, in richness and appropriateness of matter, as well as fervor in utterance." The wonder too was enhanced rather than diminished by every repetition of the exercise.

To those whose devotions Payson led for twenty years—in the sanctuary, in the prayer meeting, by the sick bed, at festivals and funerals—every prayer seemed to have the freshness of originality. His resources for this duty seemed to be absolutely inexhaustible. In his prayers was something powerful to arrest and fix attention—a something which seized and absorbed the faculties of the soul and separated it, for the time being at least, for its connections with "this present evil world." "The full, deep, reverent, flexible, suppliant tones of his voice (as far removed from the cant of the fanatic as they were from the leaven of the witling) contributed something to the effect of his public devotions." This skill in prayer, if we might call it that, came from Payson to others by the practice of long and regular retirement in the secret place. We are allowed a peep into the inner shrine; but as we tread this holy place, we feel we should take our shoes from off our feet.

It is still true that in this intercessory action of the soul "no man taketh this honor unto himself but he that is *called of God*" (Heb. 5:4). But I believe the same God that "called us, not unto uncleanness but unto holiness" calls us to intercede. Christ "offered up prayers and supplications with strong cryings and tears." This crying and tears also was known to Dr.

Payson. Lift the page of his diary and read of his "spirit of supplication," his "wrestling in prayer," his "near access to the mercy seat."

A friend writes of Payson: "Among the virtues of his character, that of humility appeared eminently beautiful and lovely and shone in his whole deportment. In prayer his soul lay low before God. Here he excelled all the men I have ever heard. He carried us up and placed us all in the divine presence; and when he spread forth his hands to God, heaven seemed to come down to earth, and the glory of the Lord shone around our tabernacle. While this holy man talked with God and seemed to be overshadowed with the divine glory, I have sometimes thought I could imagine what must have been the ecstasy of Peter when surrounded with the glories of the transfiguration scene." The emphasis again and again in Payson's life is that he was practiced in this art of intercession.

This God is our God. The God who heard the prayers of these giants in the faith—John Hyde, Charles Finney, Edward Payson—is our God. The God who listened to the lonely Elijah on Mount Carmel listens to us when we pray in the Spirit. (That last phrase is the vital part!) Giants there were! And giants there still are—mighty men who get unusual answers to prayer because they are unusual in prayer.

There is a place where thou canst touch the eyes
Of blinded men to instant perfect sight;
There is a place where thou canst say, "Arise!"
To dying captives, bound in chains of night.
There is a place where thou canst reach the store
Of hoarded gold and free it for the Lord;
There is a place upon some distant shore
Where thou canst send the worker and the Word;
There is a place where heaven's resistant power
Responsive moves to thine insistent plea;
There is a place—a silent trysting hour—
Where God himself descends and fights for thee.
Where is that secret place? Dost thou ask where?
O soul, it is the secret place of prayer!

—Author Unknown

CHAPTER FOURTEEN

"BE YE ANGRY"

The prayer records of the saints stack the vaults of heaven. What a time we shall have one day when one of the gorgeous living creatures with a mellifluous voice reads that prayer record to the assembled host! What a mighty hallelujah chorus its reading will raise. Think of the millions who have prayed, and yet how scanty are the records of deliverances wrought by a faithful God in answer to persistent believing prayers. We know that millions have proved God's power by prayer.

Prayer is another way of telling God that we have all confidence in Him but no confidence in our own native powers. Neglect of prayer is an effrontry to God, for by it we are saying that we have confidence in the flesh and can operate the spiritual life on a do-it-yourself basis. Strong men (self-strong) neglect prayer, or sometimes slight or ignore it, and therefore show their self-esteem and their near-independence of divine help. But weak men cry to God, because God's strength is guaranteed to be made perfect in their weakness. Is there one great man in the Bible—great, that is, in spiritual accomplishments—who was not a man of prayer? What do men do (all men, spiritual or otherwise) when "the roof falls in" and other helpers fail? Pray, of course. But why wait until tragedy strikes?

I was talking with one of the last missionaries to leave China after Stalin ordered the Church to leave. He spent his last night in China with some believers in their good-sized church. Sullen and silent, the Communist soldiers were standing with their backs to the walls and with their hats on. Tearfully the Chinese pastor paid tribute to the foreigners who had taught them about God. Bravely through his tears the pastor stuttered, "Why are these men here?" gesticulating with a sweep of the hand to indicate unmistakenly that he meant the Communist soldiers who were patterned against the wall. Without waiting for an answer, he went on: "They are here not because the government has failed, but because we believers have failed in prayer and witness." That was a bitter self-indictment.

So often we pray after we have fallen into the den of lions. Many times had we known the mind of the Spirit, that den need not have been ours. Because we are not yearning in prayer and burning with compassion, men are not turning to God. But men must turn or burn. We must weep or "sleep," for we can not do both. There are two commands of God: one is "Be filled with the Spirit" (a better translation is "Be being filled with the Spirit"); the other command is "Be ye angry and sin not." We seem to overlook the latter, yet it is a command equally important and as much enforced by the Spirit as the former. There is anger that is sinful, and there is an anger that is pure and without malice but filled with holy violence. The trouble with many believers is that they get angry over trifles and are unmoved about tragedies. They are angry because of some personal slight, but are sphinx-like while the wolves of lust devour our youth and while demons of false doctrine scatter the flock.

The fact that Athens was the intellectual capital of the world at that time did not move the Apostle Paul when he stopped there and walked its streets and viewed its temples. As always, he judged on the level of the spiritual, for the record says "his spirit was stirred in him, when he saw the city wholly given to idolatry" (Acts 17:16). Dr. James Moffatt translates it this way: "His soul was irritated at the sight of the idols that filled the city." The Amplified New Testament Version puts it just where I want it in this argument: "His spirit was grieved and roused to anger as he saw that the city was full of idols." Charles Kingsley Williams of England in his *New Testament in Plain English* (Dr. Tozer said that he feels this is the best of the translations outside of the King James and American Standard Versions) gives it to us in this pointed interpretation: "Now while Paul was waiting for them at Athens, it hurt him deeply to see the city full of idols."

Prayer, which often brings rest, also brings things into a sharp focus. If we are in the spirit of prayer, we no longer "see men as trees walking." We see them for what they are; we see them, as Wesley says, "with a never-dying soul to save and fit it for the skies." We see souls with an eternal content.

From the translations just given, we see that Paul's reaction to the gifted folk at Athens, still "fast bound in sin and nature's night," was one of profound concern. What would this mighty apostle feel these days if he walked down the main streets of our cities, lavishly garnished as they are with unblushing sin? Nakedness is advertized, sin glamorized, the youth mesmerized, and the church apparently paralyzed before such flagrant display of wickedness. When asked about the budget for his evangelistic operations, Dr. Billy Graham said that it was four million dollars a year, and then, before he could be beaten over the head with his own crutches, the gifted evangelist charged, "It isn't the cost of one fighter plane, or what is spent in one afternoon at a Florida race track, or on a major prize fight" (Minneapolis *Star*, July 12, 1961).

The appalling need of sinful men hit John Wesley hard on every level. He wrote, "I have two silver spoons at London and two at Bristol; this is all the plate I have at present. And I shall not buy any more while so many around me want bread" (Letter to Commissioners of Excise, September 9, 1776).

In the year that Wesley was converted, Bishop Berkley in his *Discourse to Magistrates and Men in*

Authority wrote, "Morality and religion have collapsed to a degree that has never been known in any Christian country." He continued, "Our prospect is very terrible and the symptoms grow worse from day to day." His next phrase looks as if it is off the front page of today's newspaper: "The youth born and brought up in wicked times without any bias to good from early principle or instilled opinion when they grow ripe, must be monsters indeed. And it is so to be feared that the age of monsters is not far off." The state of England in Wesley's time is versed by Samuel Johnson, the lexicographer:

> Here malice, rapine, accident conspire,
> And now a rabble rages, now a fire;
> There ambush, here relentless ruffians lay,
> And here a fell attorney prowls for prey;
> Here falling houses thunder on your head,
> And here a female atheist talks you dead.

Wesley Bready says, "The efforts of Addison, Steele, Richardson, Johnson and Goldsmith to stop this rot are like trying to get water to run uphill." The taste for the pornographic was avid; the appetite for the vulgar and the sensual was at a peak. Religion was dead.

Into this formidable, heavy arena, sin-soaked as it was, came the gallant John Wesley proclaiming, "My doctrine is not mine, but His that sent me." "A larger soul I think hath seldom dwelt in a house of clay!" spake the valet of Cromwell six months after the death of his master. We could claim the same epitaph for Wesley. To the question often asked of this sanctified Oxford don, "What made him the man he was?" we would reply, "The grace of God, plus eyes to see the lostness of men."

Just recently we heard Billy Graham in the Fair Grounds in Minneapolis thundering at the moral laxity of this day. He gave staggering statistics of illegitimate births and abortions amongst the teen-agers. As it was in the days of Noah, so also is it now. There was an ark then. Where is an ark of salvation now? We need prophets for this day of doom. The light in the prayer tower should never be put out.

We want beautiful prayers, touching prayers, simple prayers, thoughtful prayers; prayers with a quaver or a tear in them, or prayers with delicacy and dignity in them. But searching prayer, humbling prayer, which is the prayer of the conscience and not merely of the heart or taste, prayer which is bent on reality and, to win the new joy, goes through misery if need be— are such prayers as welcome and common as they should be? Too much of our prayer is apt to leave us with the self-complacency of the sympathetically incorrigible, of the benevolent and irremediable, of the breezy octogenarian, all of whose yesterdays look backward with a cheery and exasperating smile.

—P. T. Forsyth

CHAPTER FIFTEEN

THE PRAYER CHAMBER OUR MIRROR

John Greenleaf Whittier stood in speechless wonder gazing at Niagara Falls. He marvelled at the milky cataract as it hurled itself down into the canyon below and was amazed at the thunder of its waters. But he was yet more astonished when an Indian plucked his sleeve and said, "An enemy is coming!"

"How do you know?" asked Whittier.

"Because," replied the warrior, "I heard a twig break." John Whittier had heard nothing but the thundering of the waters, yet the sensitive ears of the alert hunter had heard the snapping of a twig above the roar of those raging waters.

One wonders if it is not true that in the midst of the wail of jet engines, the crash of old orders, the mesmerism of materialism, the savage competition of modern life, plus the great pull of worldly pleasure and worldly programs, we have lost an ear for the cry of millions dying "having no hope and without God in the world."

In the Introduction to his book, *In the Arena of Faith,* Erich Sauer says, "God's people need a new awakening. It is an alarming fact that in spite of the mighty voice of God in the momentous happenings of recent years, there has been no really great lasting *general* revival, not in a single European country." [1] Furthermore, Erich Sauer says, "How can we expect non-Christians to awake if we ourselves are not awakened? How can 'fire' arise if we ourselves do not 'burn'? How shall life be begotten if we ourselves are not truly filled with 'life'?" [2] Other things being equal, the outcome of union in marriage is offspring. So it is with union in Christ—life will beget life. With the Holy Spirit indwelling us, there must be the fruit of the Spirit—love, joy, peace; then, too, there will be children born in the Spirit. This much is sure: prayer warriors have entered countries that their feet never have entered and never will enter. These Spirit-illumined souls have adopted people or countries, and prayed into being, revivals and blessings that "that day" alone will reveal.

The stark-naked bankruptcy of human attributes is never more revealed than in the prayer chamber. *Outside* the prayer closet, influence, affluence, prestige and possessions hold sway and grant privilege; *inside* the secret place, all human values are negated. Muscle men and millionaires, philosophers and fighters leave all their man-made glory on the other side of the door of the prayer chamber. In this issue of prayer, what counts is holy character, obedience, and faith.

[1] Erich M. Sauer, *In the Arena of Faith,* Wm. Eerdmans Publishing Co., Grand Rapids, Mich., 1955, p. 9.
[2] Ibid., p. 10.

This race is not to the swift. This battle is not to the physically strong. The man who is rich in this world's goods has not more chance of divine favor than the man who is materially poor. Conversely then, the man who lives on the poverty line needs to fear no rejection in the prayer chamber. Thanks be unto God that this greatest of all human offices, prayer, is not contingent upon anything tarnished with materialism.

The prayer chamber is a mirror reflecting our spiritual condition. Is this why the prayer chamber is so unpopular? Do we fear self-exposure, exposure *of* ourselves *to* ourselves? Are we afraid of discovering spiritual deformity within us? The prayer chamber is the place to check up on spiritual health. Do we shun the prayer chamber lest we discover the cancer of carnality within? The prayer chamber is as a balance where we find out whether or not we are losing weight in the spiritual life. I am not thinking here of the matter of *saying* prayers but of those saints who not only "stay to pray" but who stay to listen to what God has to say to them (as well as expect God to listen to what they have to say to Him).

In this science-exalted hour when men can weigh the earth, take the temperature of the sun, and move a city in seconds, not to mention swinging men around the earth in a spaceship, man hates to find a place where his scientific knowledge is defaulted, his erudition checkmated, and his native abilities thwarted. This is why he shuns the prayer closet.

Prayer is a great revealer. Prayerless men give themselves away. Often in ministers' conferences (min-

isters are not the sole offenders here) I have seen men
kneel for about half an hour and then get up and
rub their knees as a witness that they are not used to
long prayer vigils. Men love activity, both physical
and social, but prayer calls for stillness: "Be still and
know that I am God." Men like companionship, but
prayer calls for loneliness. This is a day of "do-it your-
self" and "do-it-quickly." We have instant coffee and
instant tea. Dr. Tozer quips about instant Christians.
But there is no instant prayer. Granted that there are
times when prayer is answered like a flash and that
emergency calls get emergency answers; nevertheless,
most prayer seems to need an incubation period. (Most
of us would give God a push if we could.)

Prayer is a great beautician. Witness Moses in
his forty days and forty nights of prayer. Do you
wonder that at the end of that vigil he had a glory
upon him of which he was unconscious? We read,
"The skin of [Moses'] face shone." In Moses' case,
the marvel is that almost immediately he repeated
the forty days' fast. How did he do it?

Prayer demands strength and holy resolve. Prayer
takes strength, but also gives strength. An automobile
devalues itself every day by its use, but a violin in-
creases its mellowness with age and so enhances its
value. We are either wearing ourselves thin in Christian activity done in the flesh, or we are maturing as
we tire *in* but not *of* spiritual warfare. Let us not
easily persuade ourselves that preaching for God, or
teaching or writing for God are acceptable substitutes
to God for our omissions in prayer. Not so!

It is interesting to note that the disciples did not request, "Lord, teach us to preach." They had often heard Jesus preach; they had seen His success; they had seen how He handled the crowds. Yet they did not ask to be taught His methods but to learn His secret. They wanted to know His way of access to God, and thus they said, "Lord, teach us to pray." They saw by His example.

Example is the only real way to teach. It is one thing to instruct folk about prayer; it is quite another thing to pray. The same is true concerning teaching sacrifice and "death to self." Example is the best and really the only teacher. All else is mere philosophizing, counselling, and instructing. Christ counselled men to pray, but also led the way to the prayer chamber. Men knew He had success in prayer by the answers He got. We think of prayer very often as just "getting through" to God. It is that, I am sure; but it is equally true to say that God is trying to get through to us. God seeks for a man "to stand in the gap." *We* want to be clothed upon with power; *God* wants to strip us. *We* want power; *He* wants to expose our weakness. We want large bonuses for small investments of prayer. We want to sow radish seeds but reap a forest of redwoods. In this rush age we resent the time element in prayer and the time needed to wait for the answer, but God says, "Wait on the Lord, ... and he shall strengthen thine heart."

May I not hope that the God who came in power to eleven defeated men on the day of Pentecost, and by their means turned the world upside down, will come in power in this dark generation and do again His mighty works? —Dr. William Edwin Sangster

CHAPTER SIXTEEN

DO WE WANT ANOTHER PENTECOST?

Are we serious in saying that we want another Pentecost? We certainly *need* one, but do we really *want* one? Are we candidates for the operation of the Spirit as He comes upon us with birth pangs for a new thing to be born? There is a pattern in birth pangs. Though all babies are not alike when they are born, all babies are born the same way. One can say with accurate prediction that the coming child will be a boy *or* a girl. So there are things we can say about revival even without the wonderful gift of prophecy. The first is this: The people who experience revival will be *an obedient people*. What most of us need is not more light. Oh, no! We have far more light now than we have walked in. We are not needing more truth, for we know far more of the Bible than we have obeyed. But rather than admit this, we excuse ourselves and blame the devil. What abuse he gets from us Christians! Poor old Lucifer gets the boot for everything that goes wrong in our lives and for what we fail to get for ourselves! How expert can we get in this scapegoat mentality?

Secondly, the people who get revival will be *a humble people*. They will have not one thing in which to boast. They will bow low in the stark nakedness of their spiritual unproductiveness. My esteemed friend, Dr. Tozer, wrote an article, "The Old Cross and the New," which has winged its way around the world and has been reprinted times beyond counting. I am sometimes tempted to think that with that trenchant pen of his he could have written another article called "The Old Self and the New." The *old* self boasted of how much money it squandered, how much liquor it could hold and still drive home; it told of its ability to cheat, its skill in evil, its cunning in gambling, its brazened toiling in impurity. The *new* self talks of how far *I* have traveled, how many souls *I* have won, and how people are always wanting *me* to preach. The *new* self talks humility, but on the side groans that it was overlooked. The *new* self speaks of the Cross, but knows nothing of fasting; writes and preaches about prayer, but does as little of it as it can. Whom are we fooling? Certainly not God, for though we have sung many times, "There shall be showers of blessing," the heavens do not yield us rain.

This new self sings, "Make me little and unknown, loved and prized by Thee alone," but on the side loves to be praised and keeps all the newspaper clippings about itself. In the back of my mind I think of two men. One did exactly as I have said—kept a record of places where he had preached, noted all the decisions, and estimated the crowd. That may be all right, but— and this is the sin of it—he gloated over all *he* had done in the Lord. Vanity of vanities! Another friend, who edits a paper with a world-wide circulation, has as his favorite couplet the one mentioned above, "Make me little and unknown," but often uses page after page of that paper to tell of *his* exploits. I would laugh at the whole thing, but it is too serious for that. Oh flesh, flesh, flesh! Oh self—saved self, sanctified self—get out of God's way! We have our reward either here or hereafter, but not both times.

The tragedy is that this miserable self hinders revival, for it sabotages its own praying. (We are not a people who suffer from self-examination; introspection died with the stagecoach.) If some of us do have success, we talk as if *we* did it. But what have we that we did not receive? If we pray with one eye on success, there is no hope of revival for us, and if we are praying with an idea that *we* might be projected to the forefront, we bury every hope of revival. We must not pray for revival as a cure for the empty seats in the churches. We must not pray for a heaven-sent deluge merely to extend our particular body of believers. Prayer for revival must be pure. In pure prayer not one element of double interest can be allowed. Our first request concerning revival must be that God be glorified; *afterwards*, not before, will come our request for sinners to be saved and a believing that the heavens will be rent. God's conditions have been met.

Thirdly, before a Biblical Pentecost there must be *a praying people*, a people waiting on God. This is the pattern that has preceded every revival down the ages. Notice what the Word says: "The Lord, whom ye seek, shall suddenly come to his temple." Are we seeking the Lord? If the coming of the Lord in all His

holy power means the shattering of what is precious
to us, are we willing for this? The new wine of
revival will shatter the old wineskins of formality.

Thirty years ago I went as a youth preacher into
the island of Anglesey off the west coast of Wales.
There I met an old lady almost a hundred years of
age who told me that before Evan Roberts crossed
Telford's famous bridge into Anglesey, there were
open manifestations of the operation of the Holy Spirit
in at least five different places. When Evan Roberts
came to these places, in some cases he looked into
the church, "sensed" that God was there, and simply
said, "Obey God." To these places he never came
again for the duration of the Welsh Revival, for man
was not needed. The fact is that the pattern for all
that went before the Welsh Revival was prayer,
prayer, and more prayer.

This same pattern preceded the Moravian Revival
in the eighteenth century. The nobleman, Count Zinzendorf, learned to pray at an unusually early age. At
just sixteen when he left Halle, he handed the famous
Professor Franke a list of seven praying societies that
he had already founded. He deliberately turned from a
path of gold to care for a group of girls and teach them
the things of the Lord. Picture then this pious soul,
Zinzendorf, prostrate before God, agonizing for the
souls of a group of school girls.

Let us pause to consider: prayer for revival is no
sudden flight of fancy, no spiritual hobby. Just as no
man takes a running jump and in one leap lands on
top of the Rockies but gets there by patient toil, so

it is with prayer. Jesus said, "When thou prayest, . . . and hast shut thy door, pray to thy Father. . .and thy Father. . .shall reward thee openly." Mr. E. M. Bounds again is our mentor and he says that long praying in public is permissible only if it is preceded by long praying *in secret.*

God's Word says that when we seek the Lord, He comes to His temple. We must check here to see what it is that we who are praying for revival are seeking. We are not seeking fame, miracles, success, ease, full churches, or financial deliverance. These *may* come. But first and foremost we seek the Lord. It is He who must come in power and glory. At the transfiguration of the Lord, I think the reason Peter wanted to build three tabernacles was that he had never before seen the glory. He had heard of it with the hearing of the ear; it seems as if he finally said, "Now mine eye seeth thee." Tired of dead orthodoxy, Peter then wanted to stay where the glory was. He craved to remain in the living Presence and glory. Who can blame him?

"The Lord, whom ye seek, shall *suddenly* come." We read that when the shepherds kept watch over their flocks by night, *suddenly* there was a heavenly host saying, "Glory to God in the highest." Later, the disciples were all with one accord in the upper room and *suddenly* there was a sound as of a rushing, mighty wind. Even so with the Moravians at Herrnhut in Saxony. Zinzendorf and a little remnant were assembled together when "*suddenly* at precisely eleven o'clock in the morning on Wednesday the thirteenth of August, 1727, the Holy Ghost descended." Said Bishop

Evelyn Hasse, "When the Spirit came, was there ever in the whole of church history such an astonishing prayer meeting as that which began in 1727? It went on one hundred years and was something absolutely unique! It was known as 'The Hourly Intercession,' which meant that by relays brethren and sisters made prayer to God without ceasing for all the work and wants of His church. . . . Out of that small community more than one hundred missionaries went from them in twenty-five years." True prayer always leads to action, and in the case of the Moravians it kindled a burning desire to make Christ's salvation known to the heathen. Spirit-praying results in Spirit-directed activity.

Recently two world-famed figures committed suicide. One, a multimillionaire, threw himself from a high window of a hotel; the other, a top-line author, took a gun and shattered his head with it. There is a saturation point to all that is human. Men sin until they cannot take in any more sin. Money snares men and then reveals itself for what it is—a dead womb, unable to bring human happiness to birth. In riches men turn to despair or they turn to God. But seldom do they turn to Him to be remade by regeneration.

Folk argue that if God would move today as He has in the past, they would praise Him. But again, this is a reversal of New Testament procedure in the book of Acts, for from the ascension of Jesus to the coming down of the Spirit in the upper room, the disciples "worshipped him, and returned to Jerusalem with great joy, and were continually in the temple praising and blessing God." Here is the divine record: *Before* Pentecost they were ardent worshippers and were praising

God. Apostolic production today demands from us apostolic precedent.

What gaping holes there are in our claims to being Biblical in operation. In our church do we praise daily? Do we pray daily? Are souls added daily to our church? We want another Pentecost but in our own way. Yet we cannot mold God into our pattern: we must be shaped to *His* Biblical design. "Be ye doers of the word, and not hearers only," said the Lord.

Do we really mean business when we speak of desiring a return to apostolic Christianity? Are we expecting that it will be God who will make the first move towards revival? If a farmer had broken no ground and had spread no seed, would he be justified in blaming God because he had no harvest? With an eye on the sky we sing, "There shall be showers of blessing," hoping God on high will soon move in revival power. But aren't we like the farmer with no ground broken, no seed sown, and therefore no harvest?

Let me finish this chapter with the question that opened it: Are we serious in saying that we want another Pentecost?

There is passion in the praying that prevails. Elijah was a man of passions all compact. There was passion in all he did. All there was of him went into everything he did. God loves a man aflame. The lukewarm He cannot abide. He never keeps hot hearts waiting. "Then will I [Jehovah] be found of you when ye seek me with all your hearts." When Elijah prayed, he prayed in his prayer. Is there not much praying in which there is no prayer? The praying man [Elijah] was in his petition. Listen to his praying in the death chamber. Watch him on Carmel. Hear him plead the honor of God and cry unto the Lord for the affliction of the people. —Samuel Chadwick

CHAPTER SEVENTEEN

"I SAY THIS TO YOUR SHAME"

Napoleon Bonaparte made a lonely surprise-visit one night to the outpost sentries on one of the vital positions of his battlefield. Stealthily he moved along in the gray light of the morning. One sentry after another immediately challenged him. Finally, the crafty warrior stole up to a strategic spot. There was no sentry to challenge him. The wily Napoleon moved closer and saw a pair of boots protruding from under a shock of corn and a rifle propped beside them. He made no comment—just picked up the rifle and himself stood guard, waiting for the awakening of the snoozing soldier. Finally the corn stirred, and up jumped the guilty defender and grabbed for the gun that was gone. Can you imagine his confusion and chagrin? What a bitter and shattering experience—caught napping by *Napoleon!* When the Lord of glory returns, will He find us Christians sleeping at our post of duty? John the Apostle warns that we be not ashamed before Him at His coming.

I well remember a Bible conference in England where I stood on a platform beside a wrinkled old lady. She had a faraway look in her eyes and the drip of a tear from them too, as hundreds of people were singing:

> There is a love constraining me
> *To go and seek the lost;*
> I yield, O Lord, my all to Thee,
> To save *at any cost.*

That "elect lady," known to prisons and scarred in spiritual battle, was none other than the Maréchale, eldest daughter of William Booth, the founder of the Salvation Army. She had written the above stanza as part of a lovely hymn.

The versatility of Paul is amazing. To the Thessalonians the very same man who stormed down the road to Damascus is "as gentle as a nurse"; to the Romans he reveals the brilliance of his legal mind; and to the Corinthians he is "a wise master builder." But to Timothy, Paul is "a soldier of Jesus Christ." Years later the famed English cricketer, C. T. Studd, who deserted the playing field for the battlefield of world evangelism, used to twit folk about being what he called "chocolate soldiers." In his *Quaint Rhymes of a Quondam Cricketer*, he has this ditty:

> Get up, get up for Jesus, ye soldiers of the Cross,
> A lazy Sunday morning surely means harm and loss;
> The Church of God is calling; in duty be not slack;
> You cannot fight the good fight while lying on your back.

Let's face it: We are *not* living in a day of militant Christianity. The very suggestion throws many into a spiritual pout, for they believe the Lord did all the fighting. (Appalling philosophy!) They glibly tell me, "The battle has already been won at Calvary." Christ *did* win, but that does not eliminate human responsibility. The folly of this philosophy was burned into my mind recently while visiting tough mission fields. Men hardly expect our soldiers on earth's battle fronts to make their own ammunition as well as to fire it at the belligerent enemy. Yet on the mission battlefield we kept hearing of the lack of conquest when the folk at home cease to pray. The new missionary is snowed under with readjustments. His mind has to get readjusted to a new language; his spirit has to get readjusted to a heathen atmosphere; his appetite has to get readjusted to new foods; his soul has to get readjusted to new emotions. All things are new—new pressures he never dreamed of, new burdens he never thought of, new physical challenges. On top of these, the new missionary has to do his own sweating in prayer for victory against foes, entrenched for millenniums, who stubbornly resist ejection. All this time we at home fail to pray. We are slackers, and as far as I can discern, at the judgment seat of Christ there will be no medals for slackers. Dear reader, do you and I realize that we are just one heartbeat from a fixed state of reward, be it of joy or shame?

A missionary just wrote, "On many mission fields there is no lack of new missionaries who have technical knowledge." Of course the know-how for building, educating, and the like, is not to be despised, for there are countries right now where one cannot enter simply as a gospel missionary; he must be an artisan. Nevertheless, today the missionary cries, "We are in need of men of burning hearts, men who can knock on

doors, or trail in the bush, men motivated by holy
compassion for souls."

I do not doubt that many Christians who read
this chapter will mourn that they are not eligible for
the foreign field. Others will mourn that though they
crucified the flesh and the lusts thereof, they neglected
the bit of the text which demands crucifying the affections. There is no question that this demand for crucifixion is tough on young folk. But men who were called
to earth's battlefields crucified their affections. In the
last war, I saw rivers of tears as men left our country
for the mud and blood of the battlefield. The athlete
might come back with a shattered body, he might come
back blinded, he might come back with a flag over
him—but what of that? The risk was coolly calculated,
for England was in peril. So, tears or no tears, heartache or no heartache, sacrifice slipped out of one's
vocabulary.

But some men who once missed years of home comfort to fight on earth's battlefields will not miss even
one night's comfort now to pray for mission fields. Today there is so much physical comfort for the pray-ers.
(Our churches are more air-conditioned than prayer-
conditioned, and are well-heated too.) Not so for Master
David Brainerd. The lone forest, buried in snow, saw
him grief-stricken and brokenhearted over the lawless,
immoral, drunken Indians. Of our Saviour one wrote,

> "Long nights and chilly mountain air
> Witnessed the fervour of His prayer."

Prayer is battle. Could it be that in our churches
the right slogan over the door of most of our prayer

rooms would be "We Wrestle *Not*"? I often see listed in churches names of athletes who will play ball of some kind, but I would like to see these "muscle men" operating where strength really counts—that is, in the place of prayer. Prayer taxes even the physical frame; prayer wears on the nerves; prayer involves the whole man. Prayer *must* have priority. Prayer *must* be our bolt to lock up the night, our key to open the day. Prayer is power. Prayer is wealth. Prayer is health of the soul.

> "Prayer is the soul's sincere desire,
> Uttered or unexpressed,
> The motion of a hidden fire
> That trembles in the breast.
>
> Prayer makes the darkened clouds withdraw;
> Prayer climbs the ladder Jacob saw;
> Gives exercise to faith and love,
> Brings every blessing from above."

Shall men crippled in earthly warfare call Christians "chocolate soldiers" because we fear the gashes the enemy of souls might inflict upon us? God forbid! Shall men whose hearts once bled as they left wife and children (many with a one-way ticket) rise to our condemnation because in the greatest warfare the world has ever known, and for the greatest Captain of time and eternity, we can neither rise to pray nor skip the blankets for one night? Again I quote Scripture: "God forbid!"

When Paul the Apostle says, "Some have not the knowledge of God; I speak this to your shame," *did he mean you?*

Faith is more than belief. The devils believe and tremble, but they do not trust. Faith is trust. It is not an opinion, not a fiction, not a supposition. Faith is a faculty of vision, a process of verification, an assurance of knowledge, a logic of life. Faith demands an honest and impartial mind, a pure and disinterested motive, a loyal and steadfast obedience. This is the faith that works to the justification of the ungodly, the sanctification of the unholy, and to the mighty power that prevails in prayer. —Samuel Chadwick

CHAPTER EIGHTEEN

PRAYER AND FAITH

In a weekly series on the British Broadcasting Corporation network, a distinguished group of intellectuals who formed The Brains Trust attempted to answer high-caliber questions sent in by listeners. Professor Joad sat with this group, and whenever he was asked a question, he would invariably reply, "It just depends on what you mean by. . . ."

We say the very same thing about prayer: "It all depends on what you mean by prayer." In one sense, all people pray sometime, somewhere. But what is true prayer? We often hear people say (especially those who grudge the time that prayer demands), "It is not prayer alone that *does* things." We heartily concur with this view, for first of all, prayer is tied to obedience, and then to faith and claiming the promises. A parachutist falling through the air is not safe just because he reads the instruction, "Pull the rip cord." Neither is he safe because he knows the rip cord is there. He is safe only when he obeys the sign, acts upon his knowledge, and pulls the cord. This is the reason the Scripture says that knowing these things is not enough. "Happy are ye *if ye do them.*" We sabotage much of our praying by disobedience.

Here is a man with a conviction that he should fast. But this is the rub—he fears that if he does fast, his wife will upbraid him and cry out that he will impair his health. (Most of us would be healthier if we did fast; even some health clubs are insisting on certain fastings.) However, in the matter of fasting, a Christian's own opinion does not count, and his wife's opinion does not count either. The court of appeal here, as in other spiritual matters, is "What saith the Scriptures?"

It must be right to say that in the hearts of those men privileged to walk with the Master, prayer thirst was created for the very reason that when Jesus prayed, things happened.

Colton said, "Pure truth, like pure gold, has been found unfit for circulation because men have discovered that it is far more convenient to adulterate the truth than to refine themselves. They will not advance their minds to the standards; therefore they lower the standards to their minds."

Would it be irrelevant to apply this searching test to the ministry of the Word? Frankly, are there not things in the Scriptures that are out of the reach of many of us? Whereas Colton spoke of men advancing their minds to the standards, we Christians might talk of men adjusting their lives and hearts to the requirements of Scripture in order that in this evil day out-of-reach blessings and miracles may happen.

The Book says, "Without faith it is impossible to please [God]." Often we hear it said, "*All men* have faith," and to bolster up this argument a case like this is cited: Here is a man boarding an airplane. He does not ask to see the pilot's flying license; he does not check on the plane's certificate of airworthiness. Soon he is ripping through the skies. The plane banks, twists and turns, yet the passenger does not bother to ask if the pilot is off course. He just sits. Why? "Because," says our informant, "he has faith in the pilot." But that is hardly a right analogy. In the back of the traveler's mind he knows the government demands that the pilot be capable, that the plane be airworthy, and that it have a predetermined destination. What the passenger really has is natural faith, which has no value at all in the spiritual realm.

Paul makes it very clear that all men have not faith (II Thess. 3:2). And again, God says, "Faith is the gift of God." It seems to me that a soul often escapes "the net" when an altar call is given because he already has evaded every argument the preacher put forward. The preacher has rightly laid on a heavy argument about sin, but his listener pronounced his own absolution "because," says he, "I have not done those things which the preacher spoke of." In other words, the listener is saying, "I am *not* bad." Yet God's first argument with a man is not that he is bad but that he is "dead." God says, "You hath he quickened *who were dead in. . . sins.*" The first step to recovery in spiritual life, then, is repentance toward God. I have so often heard folk at the altar bemoaning their lack of faith. Well they might, for they have none. God says so! Therefore, let the sinner who is dead in sins, repent. This is the gateway to blessing, and upon this act of obedience faith will be the gift of God. From there on, every believer is a joint-heir with Christ, an heir of the resources of a limitless God.

In the New Testament, faith is mentioned some 340 times. Strangely enough, whereas all the heroes of faith in Hebrews eleven are Old Testament characters, yet in the whole of the Old Testament, faith is mentioned only twice (Deut. 32:20; Hab. 2:4).

In Paul's first letter to the Thessalonians, he commented favorably on their faith. He was not accusing them of having no faith but of having an undeveloped faith. He had great anxiety for them that they might "perfect that which was lacking in their faith." His prayer for the Thessalonians was answered, for see how he speaks about their faith in his second letter: "We are bound to thank God for you, . . . because that your faith groweth exceedingly" (II Thess. 1:3). The faith that had previously been stalled in them was now spoken of in a superlative way.

Faith can grow. If we would please God, faith must grow. Faith is supersensory. It does not cling to logic; it does not have to abide by logic; it does not have to fear to be judged by logic. Faith can lie dormant for a while (as in the Thessalonians), but then can be ignited and stirred to "lay hold of God." We are not to have faith in our faith, but faith in the finished work of Christ and in the promises of God. We can have the faith of Christ because Paul says, "The life which I now live in the flesh, I live *by the faith of the Son of God*," and again, "Christ liveth *in me.*" The Christ, who in the days of His flesh himself believed His Father, made it possible for the Apostle to believe the Father, for the reason that Christ lived in Paul. Such a truth is beyond any logic that the world knows.

In Auckland, New Zealand, we had refreshment for body, and inspiration for spirit in the delightful home of the Ivor Davies. One day Ivor told me of a time when he and his family were forced to vacate a house they were occupying. They had not been in New Zealand long, and now there was a deadline for vacating the house rented. To take a common sense view and store the furniture would have been easy. (We are all skilled in rationalizing.) Yet Ivor and his wife refused to store it and ordered a furniture van. Then its driver wanted to know where the load was going. Ivor did not know. The men continued to load the van, and before the operation was quite complete, a person in another area offered them a house for immediate use. Hallelujah!

Look at that crowd singing

"Faith, simple faith, the promise sees
    And looks to God alone;
    Laughs at impossibilities
    And cries, 'It shall be done.' "

It is that phrase, "Looks to God alone," that jars. We want to do something ourselves and then let God take a hand. (Abraham tried to help God fulfill the promise of a son, and today we suffer from the result.)

I remember a Christian group in England who, when they doubled their membership by a merger, had great rejoicing over the result. Many began to say, "This merging is a work of the Lord." But one bold brother questioned the whole thing. "It is," he ventured to say, "just like the merger which the super stores are making today"—meaning, I think, that there was not a sign of anything supernatural about it. In my judgment he was right, even though what he had said later cost him his job with that church group. But even that action did not prove this brother to be wrong.

I am convinced beyond a shadow of a doubt that a supernatural manifestation is what not only those in the world want to see, but also what many in the church are pining to see. Many of God's dear people read the Scriptures with an uneasy mind, knowing that in their own lives when it comes to miracles and manifestations which are beyond rationalization, it is *not* true that "as he is, so are we in this world." Perhaps they are like Gideon, who when told that the Lord was with him, said, "If the Lord is with us... *where be all his miracles* which our fathers told us of?" As far as Gideon was concerned, miracle was in the past tense.

Is it not unpardonably true that most of us explain our Christian life this way: "I don't drink or smoke or swear or gamble or dance or lust or steal, etc."? Good as these negations are, they are not enough. There is one faith, one true Christian faith; all other faiths, however charming and seductive and successful they may be, are false. At times I am tempted to be cynical when we well-dressed, well-fed, well-housed people sing, "Faith of our fathers," and go on to sing, "How sweet would be their children's fate if they like them *could die* for Thee." As I see it, folk with a shattered prayer life, folk who can hardly be dragged to a mid-week prayer meeting, would never be candidates for a martyr's crown.

There is certainly a faith to defend, a faith "once for all delivered to the saints." But we are thinking of active faith. There is a faith which we have as a "fruit of the Spirit." Even the regenerate soul should have this blessed fruit. And, dear reader, remember that faith, like fruit, grows, ripens, and then produces its kind. There is also a faith which is listed as a "gift of the Spirit" (I Cor. 12:9). And there is a rest of faith. Faith does *not* have to struggle and fret; faith can rest. (There may be wrestlings against principalities and powers, but that is another matter.) Faith laughs at impossibilities and cries, "It shall be done."

Through the channel of faith comes all that we have or ever will have in the Christian life this side of eternity.

The majority of us saints are sound asleep to the devastation going on, and we shall come under the bitter curse of Meroz if we do not rouse ourselves up and stand with God against the mighty.

—Oswald Chambers

The enemy is today more bold, more open, more defiant, more determined than any army general, I believe, in the past has ever had any experience of; and to know that there is an enemy is half the battle. He was no myth to the Lord Jesus Christ. He is no myth in the Bible, and we have no right to leave people in ignorance of him and his workings today.   —Gordon Watt

CHAPTER NINETEEN

CONCERNING ZEAL

That a woman had a baby is no miracle. The fact that the lady is Mrs. Chumbi adds no luster to the event either. But wait a minute. Last February a strike cancelled our plane reservation from New Delhi, and because of this, Pan-American gave us fine accommodations in the luxurious Royal Imperial Hotel. Then, what seemed to be a provocation turned out to be a providence, for it was at New Delhi that I met Mrs. Chumbi, introduced by the caption in the newspaper, *The Statesman.*

Her story went like this: Around the latter part of February 1961, her Majesty, Elizabeth, Queen of England, was to be in Katmandu, the capital of Nepal. Khunjo and Mrs. Chumbi, who live in a village near Mt. Everest, were invited to the royal reception. On the fifteenth day of February Mr. and Mrs. Chumbi set off for the royal party, organized miles away in Katmandu. (Mr. Chumbi is the new keeper of the famed Yeti scalp: he found a withered arm which he claims is the remains of the "abominable snowman.")

Picture then the rough road that these two walked. Imagine if you can that they actually covered the intervening distance (numbering 180 miles) in ten days. *Good* going by any standard! *Great* going for a gentle lady! *Magnificent* going for a lady expecting a baby any day! Six days away from Katmandu, this incredible woman was in great pain. Let the newspaper tell the simple tale just here: "She sat down calmly by the roadside and gave birth to a son. Then after about an hour's rest, she got up and walked on with the Sherpa party." Think of it—one hour after confinement, Mrs. Chumbi roused herself and kept up the fast pace to the capital, afraid that she might be late to see the queen. Zeal drove this couple over the hazards and flinty roads of the Himalayas in order to see and shake hands with the famous queen.

This burst of admiration and affection for the queen is quite legitimate, and by many it is even commended. Likewise the enthusiasm among sport fans. When some fanatics in sport sit all night outside an English football ground in the shivers and snow in order that they may be sure of getting a ticket to see a cup-tie in English soccer, the crowd sings lustily, "He's a jolly good fellow." Only when we show zeal in spiritual matters, folk term us "nutty." Spiritual zealots are so rare these days that if one turns up in our ranks, he either gets a dousing from everybody's theological hosepipe or hits the opposite extreme and gets a book written about him. It's a hose or a halo for the zealot!

In Christian circles, zeal is just about taboo. But with the Communists, zeal is not only expected; it is encouraged. The J. W.'s merit the title "blind leaders of the blind," but when we see their untiring efforts to proselytize, we have to give them credit. They compass land and sea to make their captives seven times more the children of hell than they are themselves. Before the doorstep can cool from the J. W.'s, the Mormons are on it. Both schools of zealots turn out devotees with one-track minds whose perverted thinking can be toppled with a few Bible verses, some prayer, and a little zeal. The reason for the success of these cults is not that they have more to offer than others or that they offer what they have in a more attractive or convincing way. The J. W.'s and the Mormons score by persistence. The dupes of these cult merchants interpret zeal as personal interest or love. Folk are lonely, despite Lonely Heart clubs or the ever-chatting radio or the flashing TV. The vacuum within is eloquent in its silence. A famed psychologist says that everybody's problem over forty years of age is a spiritual one.

With all the Apostle Paul's greatness and staggering theological knowledge, he was happy to get on doorsteps and strike the door knocker (Acts 20:20). We might well emulate the great preacher in that. I am sure that many believers, who might have a river of joy if they did but activate themselves in some form of personal evangelism, are trying to steal a spoonful of happiness from a TV show. But no money has yet been minted that can buy true joy. It is the by-product of devoted service and is purest and strongest when that service is for the Lord of glory. Put zeal into Christian service and out comes joy.

The Apostle Paul stated that Israel had "a zeal of God but not according to knowledge" (Rom. 10:2). I wonder how many of us might come under condemnation there. David says, "The zeal of thine house hath eaten me up" (Ps. 69:9), for he was consumed with zeal for the glory of the Lord. Years later, after the Master had driven out the moneychangers, the Apostle John in his Gospel adds, "His disciples remembered that it was written, The zeal of thine house hath eaten me up."

Unholy zeal made Barabbas a murderer; holy zeal made Paul a messenger and martyr for the cause of the Lord he so zealously followed. Ray Palmer's fine words come to mind right here. Everyone of us might well sing them with new devotion:

> May Thy rich grace impart
> Strength to my fainting heart,
> *My zeal inspire.*
> As Thou hast died for me,
> So may my love to Thee
> Pure, *warm*, and changeless be
> A living fire.

I hope Mrs. Chumbi is feeling better now. I feel better for the challenge that her devotion to her Queen gave me. Oh that we might say in truth what the Lord says of himself: "[I] was clad with zeal as a cloke" (Isa. 59:17)!

One poor soul entered the school of prayer after his arrival in hell. He asked for relief from his agony; it was refused. He asked that a beggar warn his brothers; he was turned down. He was praying to Abraham, a man; he could not locate God. He dared not ask to get out; he plainly knew that he was beyond all hope. Prayerless on earth, unanswered in hell, he suffers on as the man who tried to learn to pray too late.

—Cameron V. Thompson,
The Master Secrets of Prayer

CHAPTER TWENTY

SOW IN PRAYER—REAP IN POWER

It must be obvious to the reader, unless he has totally misread our motive in this writing, that we are aiming here at a state of prayer far beyond using God as a means of escape or relief. The state of praying that we seek is free from all personal request for personal benefit. We are seeking a love for the will of God among men, for the manifestation of the power of God among men, and for the recovery of the glory of God among men.

The language of the Spirit can never be reduced to writing, for the burdens of the Holy Ghost defy analysis. Such is the mystery of a Spirit-burden that at the times when we would know it, it cannot be found; and often when least expected, it comes upon us with crushing power. One trick of the Evil One is to get us to wait until we feel like praying. But if the life-boat man, having heard a distress signal from a sinking boat, waited until he felt like going to the rescue, would he not be classed as a shirker and a coward? Feelings or no feelings, we *must* pray.

Dr. P. T. Forsyth, one time Dean of the Faculty of Theology in the University of London, used to

say, "It is truer to say that we live the Christian life
in order to pray than that we pray in order to live
the Christian life." But there are degrees of life: the
baby has life; the youth has life; men of middle age
have life; the aged have life. Yet what differences of
power in life these groups manifest. So it is spiritually.
All who are born again of the Spirit of God have life
through the Son. But some who have been born again
have gone on with the Lord and received the Spirit's
fullness. Still others have matured in that fullness
into the life of intercession.

John Smith of the quiet hamlet of Cudworth near
Barnsley, England, is an example of an intercessor.
He excelled in piety and gloried in prayer. He was
given to long hours of intercession and knew the worth
of souls. Hear him: "Perhaps you will have to spend
hours on your knees or upon your face before the
throne. Never mind. Wait. God will do great things
for you if you will wait for Him. Yield to Him. Co-
operate with Him. Oh play the man! Dwell in the
clear light."

John Smith knew of sudden visitations of the Spirit.
At times these "enduements" came in the very middle
of a meal as a test in order to see whether he would
satisfy the flesh and its appetite or cleave to the horns
of the altar. He did the latter. I peep into the records
and read what Richard Treffry, Jr., says of John Smith:
"While at supper, Mr. Methley opened the business;
John Smith, laying down his knife and fork, listened
with the most patient and respectful attention. But as
soon as the former had ceased, Smith burst into a
flood of tears and literally sobbing with grief, at length

replied, 'What you say is all correct. I ought to put restraint on myself; but oh, how can I? God has given me such a sight of perishing souls that I am broken-hearted and can only vent my feelings in the way I do, entreating souls to come to God and pleading with God to act upon them and save them.' Still weeping as in an agony, he continued, 'Look around you, my brother, and do you not see sinners going to hell? And when I thus see and feel it, I am compelled to act.'

"To this pathetic statement there was no reply. All the company was melted into tears, and Mr. Methley was so deeply affected that, unable to restrain his emotions, he abruptly rose from the table and left the house."

Yet again in writing to a friend of John Smith he says, "I have often seen him come downstairs in the morning after several hours in prayer, his eyes swollen with weeping. He would soon introduce the subject of his anxiety by saying, 'I am a brokenhearted man; yes, indeed, I am an unhappy man, not for myself but on account of others. God has give me such a sight of the value of precious souls that I cannot live if souls be not saved. Oh give me souls, or else I die!' "

John Smith was typical of other early Methodist preachers who jealously guarded their prayer life. David Stoner, a contemporary of Smith (indeed he was born the same year), was another Methodist preacher who was devoted and disciplined in prayer and who blazed a trail of revival for God in England. Time would fail me to tell of Bramwell, Bradford.

Nelson, and a host of other men of like passions with Smith.

Today this habit of prayer is not shut up to one denomination nor yet to one generation. Sick as the Church is these days, one is cheered to find those who still seek the face of the Lord in long hours of intercession. Happily, these too are scattered by the Spirit throughout the various believers and denominations.

In concluding this book my final appeal is for pastors of churches to set a prayer pattern. Let me quote from old Thomas Manton (1750): "Like priests, like people; O ye ministers of the Word, consider well that you are the first sheets from the king's press. Others are printed after your copy. If the first sheet be well set, a thousand more are stamped with ease. See, then, that the power of religion prevail over your own hearts, lest you not only lose your own souls but cause the ruin of others."

Let Spurgeon express himself on this thought: "Correction for the press is work that has to be done with great care since thousands of copies will be faulty if the proof sheet be not as it should be. So the minister of a congregation should be seriously earnest to be right because his people will imitate him. *Like priest, like people*. The sheep will follow the shepherd. What need there is that the pastor should order his steps aright lest he lead a whole flock astray! If the town clock be wrong, half the watches in the place will be out of time."

These then are words of wisdom from men of another day who were themselves models of piety. When the pastor prays, the church prays. Augustine of the fifth century said that if he could have three wishes granted, one would be to have heard the Apostle Paul preach. I too would love that privilege, but rather would I choose to have heard that great apostle to the Gentiles *pray*.

Those favored to get their souls drenched under the prayer power of God's workman, John Hyde, never forgot the mighty experience. One of the few thus blest leaves this record: "As he [John Hyde] came before the people. . . he spoke three words in Urdu and three in English, repeating them three times: 'Ai Asmani Bak, Oh, Heavenly Father.' What followed, who can describe? It was as if a great ocean came sweeping into that assembly. Hearts were bowed before that Divine Presence as the trees of the wood before a mighty tempest. It was the ocean of God's love being outpoured through one man's obedience. Hearts were broken before it. There were confessions of sins, with tears that were soon changed to joy, and then to shouts of rejoicing. Truly, we were filled with new wine, the new wine of heaven."

One wonders why this is such an isolated experience in the Church today. True prayer is Spirit-born. True prayer is praying "in the Holy Ghost." Those filled with the Spirit are filled with prayer. There is something very questionable and unbiblical about those who claim a baptism of the Spirit and yet know nothing of extended periods in prayer. I am sure Jesus prayed before the Spirit descended upon Him at the Jordan, though there is no record of it. After He was endued, He went into the wilderness. There, every battering that His Spirit could know hammered upon His naked soul and mind. But notice this: He "returned in the power of the Spirit into Galilee." He returned not in exhaustion but in power—more than conqueror.

We are in a tough spiritual battle these days. Yet the church that prays will be a prevailing church. Praying in secret means prevailing in public. One of the powerhouses of the church in America has been the camp meeting. Alas, many of these are changing and not for the better. One Sunday night I attended a great camp meeting which over 3,000 people attended. Next day fewer than 300 were present. With a sigh a minister said, "This is becoming a 'Drive-In' camp meeting." By the mercy of God we need to stay in the atmosphere of Christian fellowship and of the brooding of the Holy Spirit. One could wish that more time could be given to prayer in the camp meetings. In my opinion it would be a gilt-edged investment if any denomination definitely alloted one camp meeting a year to instruction in prayer and in the exercise of prayer. Surely for this type of ministry the crowds would not come. But the Lord would come! And if He were obeyed, the glory would come, and vision would come, and every church represented at such a meeting would be mightily enriched.

Revival can be brought to this generation by prayer, by faith, by cleansing, and by obedience to the will of God.